informationnationwarrior

Information Management Compliance
boot camp

RANDOLPH A. KAHN, ESQ. & BARCLAY T. BLAIR

Praise for *Information Nation Warrior*

Information Nation Warrior provides a practical and comprehensive template for reducing risk in today's increasingly regulated and litigious business environment. With the realities of Sarbanes-Oxley, more active regulators, and the trials and tribulations of e-discovery, there has never been a greater need for organizations to take control of their information assets. And there has never been a greater demand for an approach that applies across all levels of an organization because, more so than with any other legal issue, information management compliance requires the appreciation and participation of every employee. *Warrior* will help all parts of your organization understand and address their compliance responsibilities."

Jay Cohen, Global Compliance Leader, D&B

Informative, thought provoking, and at times entertaining, *Information Nation Warrior* provides a roadmap for collaboration between IT, legal, business and RM to achieve information management compliance. Once again, the Kahn and Blair team serves up endless ammunition to get the job done.

Jeanne B. Caldwell, CRM

Information Nation Warrior is a book every executive, senior leader, CIO, IT professional, legal counsel, records manager, and anyone who has responsibility for developing and managing information systems needs to read and understand. It is an authoritative and powerful "how-to book" for people who individually and collectively must lead their organizations to achieve information management compliance. I will be strongly recommending it in my consulting, executive briefings, seminars, and publications.

> *Dr. Mark Langemo, CRM; Professor Emeritus, College of Business and Public Administration, University of North Dakota; veteran information management author, consultant, and seminar leader*

In *Information Nation Warrior*, Kahn and Blair address the challenges facing those responsible for information management today. *Warrior* discusses how IT, Legal, Business, and Records Management issues are intertwined, and how the Warrior must strive to address them all in a coordinated way. The book points the way to the future of information management compliance, but begs the question of who will step forward and lead their organization. Kahn and Blair have laid it out—now it's up to readers to accept the challenge.

> *Jenny R Jolinski, CRM; CDIA+; Manager, Corporate Records, Darden Restaurants (parent company of Red Lobster, Olive Garden, etc.)*

Information Nation Warrior is an excellent resource for anyone responsible for information management compliance in their company. *Warrior* provides concepts that can help individuals move their organizations from theory to practice.

> Sandra Behel, Ph.D., Manager of Corporate Records and
> Library Services, Energen Corporation

Information Management Compliance means understanding the convergence of IT, Legal, Business, and Records Management requirements. *Information Nation Warrior* offers readers the view from each of these areas, leaving them better prepared to ask the right questions, properly delegate roles, and provide greater value to their organizations.

> Gene Stavrou, Records Management Program Manager, Altria
> Corporate Services, Inc. (services company of Altria Group,
> parent of Kraft Foods, Philip Morris International, and Philip
> Morris USA)

An incredibly provocative book that is especially good at raising the key issues that must be faced in today's legally-driven information environment.

> Tom Allman, Senior Counsel, Mayer, Brown, Rowe & Maw
> (Chicago); former General Counsel, BASF Corporation

Other Books from the Authors

From Randy Kahn
   Information Nation: Seven Keys to Information Management Compliance
   E-Mail Rules: A Business Guide to Managing Policies, Security, and Legal Issues for E-Mail and Digital Communication

From Barclay Blair
   Information Nation: Seven Keys to Information Management Compliance
   Secure Electronic Commerce (Editor)
   Professional XML (Editor)

informationnationwarrior
Information Management Compliance
boot camp

AIIM

Silver Spring, Maryland,
United States

Worcester, United Kingdom

RANDOLPH A. KAHN, ESQ. & BARCLAY T. BLAIR

The authors have taken care in the researching and writing of this book. However we make no warranties of any kind and assume no responsibility for any mistakes, errors, misinterpretations, or omissions. Given the evolving legal and technical environments in which this book was drafted, the contents of the book may be time limited. In any event, before taking any action in response to any material contained in the book, please consult a professional to address your particular question or issue. The authors do not assume any responsibility or liability in any way arising out of or in connection with this book.

This publication is intended to provide authoritative and accurate information regarding its topic, but is sold with the understanding that neither the authors nor the publisher are engaged in providing legal advice or other professional services. Those requiring legal advice or the assistance of experts should consult a competent professional.

Library of Congress Cataloging-in-Publication Data
Kahn, Randolph.
Information nation warrior : an information management
compliance boot camp / Randolf A. Kahn, and Barclay T. Blair.
p. cm.
Includes bibliographical references.
ISBN 0-89258-408-4 (alk. paper)
1. Management information systems--United States. 2. Information technology--United States--Management. 3. Business records--Data processing--Management. 4. Business records--Law and legislation--United States. 5. Disclosure of information--Law and legislation--United States. I. Blair, Barclay T. II. Title.
HD30.213.K345 2005
658.4'038--dc22   2005008426

Design by Jane Firor & Associates, Cover illustration by Vanessa Sifford, Production by OmniStudio, and Printing by Port City Press/ Cadmus

Special discounts on bulk quantities of AIIM publications are available upon request. For details, contact AIIM Publications, 1100 Wayne Avenue, Suite 1100, Silver Spring, MD, 20910, U.S., 301-587-2711. www.aiim.org

Dedications

The term "Warrior" and related concepts are used in a strictly metaphorical way throughout this book. However, the authors recognize that today there is an ongoing battle that is all too real, and wish to acknowledge the sacrifices made by those working across the globe to protect the innocent and advance the cause of liberty and democracy.

Randolph A. Kahn, ESQ.

To Melissa, Dylan, Lily and Teddy.

To Pop, for teaching me so much about how to conduct my life.

Barclay T. Blair

To Margie.

To my parents, Bob and Brenda, for helping me to realize that understanding is not a prerequisite for love.

Table of Contents

This book is a guide for the Information Nation Warrior. Who or what is an Information Nation Warrior? A Warrior is anyone who shares responsibility for the development, implementation, management, and administration of an information management policy or program.

Warriors include people like:

- An IT system administrator drafting an email, privacy, or security policy
- A finance executive working on Sarbanes-Oxley compliance
- An information security officer auditing data security practices
- An HR professional providing feedback on the company's electronic communications policy
- A lawyer grappling with how to efficiently deal with electronic discovery
- A manager performing an audit of her department's adherence to the email or records management policy
- A compliance officer auditing the firm's compliance program
- An in-house attorney reviewing a records retention schedule created by an outside consultant
- A records manager updating the company's records management policies and practices to address electronic records
- A sales executive evaluating a new customer relationship management system
- A storage administrator evaluating a new storage system
- A sales manager improving the way that customer data, sales leads, invoices, and contracts are handled
- A line-of-business executive participating in a records management policy drafting committee

Warriors come to the world of information management from a variety of backgrounds, but they all need a similar base of knowledge in order to do their jobs and communicate with other

Warriors throughout the organization. This book is designed to help diverse Warriors establish that common base of knowledge.

Information Nation Warrior is divided into four main parts, with each part, or Quadrant, representing an area of knowledge that the Warrior requires. Some Warriors may already have expertise in one or more Quadrants, whereas other Warriors may be completely new to Information Management Compliance (IMC) and need grounding in each Quadrant.

This book is written so that readers may focus on those areas of most use to them, and may skip or skim those sections where they have existing expertise. However, each Quadrant contains not only information that is relevant to readers without expertise in that Quadrant, but also discusses common failures, oversights, and other issues that will be helpful to all. So, for example, although an attorney may want to focus first on the IT, Business, and Records Management Quadrants, she will also likely find the Legal section of value as well.

Information Nation Warrior is a companion book to *Information Nation: Seven Keys to Information Management Compliance*. *Information Nation* is a guidebook for **organizations**; it introduces and explores the concept of IMC in detail, and discusses what organizations should do in order to address their IMC needs. Information Nation Warrior is a guidebook for **individuals** to understand their role in their organization's IMC.

Although this book and *Information Nation* are complementary, reading *Information Nation* is not a prerequisite to understanding and benefiting from this book.

Preface

By John F. Mancini

Elephants and Information Management Compliance

> *Once upon a time, there were four blind men who had the opportunity to experience an elephant for the first time. The first walked toward the elephant and, upon encountering one of its sturdy legs, announced "Ah, an elephant is like a tree." The second man first grabbed the trunk and proclaimed, "No, an elephant is like a strong hose." The third, playing with an ear, stated "You don't know what you are talking about. An elephant is more like a fan." And the last leaned against the side of the animal and said with equal conviction, "An elephant is like a wall." They all then began to argue vociferously about who had the most accurate perception of the elephant. The argument lasted long into the night.*
>
> —Old Indian Proverb

Managing information has never been more challenging. Every day, each of us encounters aspects of the information management "elephant" within our organizations. Sorting through this information and separating the critical from the mundane is increasingly a challenge.

To make the problem even more daunting, like the blind men, none of us has a complete picture of the full dimensions of the elephant. We each bring to the task of information management our assumptions and biases and experiences—and our narrow personal information requirements. Seldom do we step back and systematically think through the question of what our *organization* needs—to keep our processes running, to stay in compliance with cascading government regulatory demands and requirements, to respond to customer inquiries, or simply to make sure that we don't wind up on a witness stand.

Some would view this kind of holistic view of information management as a luxury. I would argue that in the last few years, it has moved from being a "nice to have" to a business *necessity*. We are in the middle of a revolution in business documentation. We have clearly left the safe old world of paper-based records. Most of us find ourselves in a curious no-man's land in which decisions and processes are documented with an odd patchwork quilt of paper, email, PDFs, Word files, images, spreadsheets, web sites, and data.

Describing this landscape was the primary mission of AIIM's first collaborative effort with Randy Kahn and Barclay Blair, *Information Nation: Seven Keys to Information Management Compliance*. The mission of this new book is to help individuals *within* organizations understand their unique contributions—and responsibilities—in shaping a new strategy toward the management of information.

This book looks at information management from four critical perspectives—IT, legal, business, and records management. It is intended to help executives from each of these four disciplines develop a personal roadmap for Information Management Compliance—to help them become Information Management *Warriors*.

In many ways, the mission of this book mirrors the mission of AIIM. AIIM, the international authority on Enterprise Content Management (ECM), is leading the way to the understanding, adoption, and use of the technologies, tools, and methods associated with managing documents, content, and business processes. ECM tools and technologies provide solutions to help users with four key business drivers: continuity, collaboration, regulatory compliance, and reduced costs.

In reading this book, please do not hesitate to ask how AIIM can help in your own efforts to become an Information Management Warrior. AIIM's constituency is unique in many ways because our membership matches almost exactly the four disciplines in this book—IT, legal, business, and records management. Among the various organizations that operate within the document, content, and records arena, only AIIM is positioned to bring together these four critical disciplines. Let us know how we can help.

The task before all of us is not easy. It is *never* easy being in the middle of a revolution. Another old proverb—this one Chinese—says "May you be cursed to live in interesting times." And these are interesting times indeed for those responsible for the documentation of organizational decisions and processes. This book represents an important element in helping executives navigate through these interesting times—and hopefully avoid a trampling by the elephant.

John F. Mancini
President, AIIM

Acknowledgements

Author's Acknowledgements

We have benefited enormously from the support and encouragement of our friends and colleagues who contributed to this book in many ways, including volunteering their valuable time to provide feedback on the manuscript.

For this we wish to sincerely thank:

Jay Cohen, Jeanne B. Caldwell, Dr. Mark Langemo, Jenny R. Jolinksi, Sandra Behel, PhD., Gene Stavrou, Tom Allman, and Joanna Blackburn.

Special thanks to Thomas Flynn for his invaluable contribution, insight, and perseverance.

The Information Nation Warrior: An Introduction

It's a sunny Friday afternoon and you're sitting at your desk, wondering if you should slip out a bit early to beat the traffic. Suddenly, your boss appears. He has a concerned look on his face. He makes a bit of small talk, and then out it comes:

> *"I was reading the Business Journal this morning and there was a story about a class action lawsuit filed by a group of customers who say that an online retailer charged them for a bunch of stuff they didn't order. The customers say they clicked 'no' on a pop-up window, but the company says they clicked 'yes.' Is that something that could ever happen to us?"*

After valiantly fighting the temptation to simply say, "No, of course not," and enjoy a peaceful weekend, what is the right response?

Can you answer the question? If so, what kind of guidance can you provide? Where do you go for the information you need? Who do you talk to? Is there a clear answer?

If you are in information technology (IT), you might respond with an explanation of how the Web works, how your website is structured, and how capturing a user's "click" on a "Buy Now" button all depends on the script that is used. But do you know how long this information is retained, if it is retained at all, where it is retained, and whether or not the courts would consider it acceptable evidence?

If you are an attorney, you might explore the general acceptance of "click-wrap" or "click-through" agreements, or you might answer that case law around such issues is constantly evolving and it is difficult to predict precisely what may happen in a given case in a given jurisdiction. But have you ever talked to IT about how they structured and built your website and why they made the decisions they did?

If you are a business manager, you might talk about how the website is structured to provide the user with a seamless user experience and to minimize the number of times a user has to click in order to buy. But did you ever run the design of the website by the company's attorney and get her feedback on privacy, electronic contracting, and other issues?

If you are in records management, you might reply that you are in the process of updating the retention schedule to address all types of electronic information and, once that is completed, webpages will be included in the schedule. But does IT have any idea that the retention schedule exists and have you talked to them about the tools that might be needed to capture and store this kind of information?

In all likelihood, neither you nor anyone else in your organization could provide a complete answer to this question on your own. The answer is complex and requires a combination of IT, legal, business, and records management expertise. It requires a breadth of knowledge and training that any one professional in any of those areas likely does not possess.

An organization's ability to correctly anticipate and answer questions like this one increasingly means the difference between winning and losing when it comes to information management. As a result, individuals from all areas of the enterprise are today being asked to play a greater role in the development, implementation, and administration of information management programs.

So, how do you answer your boss's question?

The very fact that she is asking **you** the question means that—like it or not—you have a new line in your job description. You are being asked to bring your background and expertise to bear on new information management challenges. There are some areas of information management that you have a good grasp on and others where you have gaps. You need to step back and understand the information management challenge in a holistic way. You need to know who to talk to, where to go, and how to get answers to help you succeed.

You need to become an Information Nation Warrior.

"Policies exist, are continually updated, but not strictly enforced."

"Management has a hard time keeping up with changing technology that is put in place."

"We have a long way to go. There is no formal policy across the organization."

Information Management Compliance Survey,
AIIM International and Kahn Consulting, Inc., April 2004

A senior engineer at a large manufacturing company is fired. The engineer, believing that he was treated unfairly, sues for wrongful termination. In preparing for the trial, the engineer requests that his former employer produce thousands of email messages and related digital documents relevant to his case.

The judge orders the company to produce the information. However, much of the email is months old, has been moved off the company's active systems, and only exists on backup systems. To make matters worse, the company discovers that many of the relevant backup tapes have been overwritten as part of a routine tape recycling procedure.

The company is forced to go back to the judge and tell her that most of the email requested has been destroyed, and that it will cost thousands of dollars to recover the remainder. The judge is not pleased. She views the company's failure to preserve and produce the digital evidence as irresponsible, a violation of an obligation to the court that, at the least, unfairly impacts the other litigant. In fact, she takes the view that the failure was part of a deliberate attempt to destroy incriminating evidence, thereby frustrating the judicial process.

She sanctions the company and rules for the engineer. The firm takes a seven-figure hit.

The company is stunned. It conducts a "what went wrong?" audit, and finds out that:

- The records management coordinator in the engineering department had published a policy that addressed the retention of email messages. However, employees had received no training or tools to actually enable them to comply with the policy. That was planned in the next budget cycle.

- In-house counsel had prepared a "Legal Hold" notice describing how information should be managed in the event of litigation, but it had only been distributed to some attorneys, a records manager, and a few employees.

- The email administrator in IT thought that as long as he had a written backup plan and stuck to it, he was avoiding any legal problems.

- For months the fired engineer's boss had been "papering the file" on the engineer, preparing for the day he may need to take action. The boss kept this meticulously organized treasure trove of email and other digital documents on a shared network drive that only he knew about.

- There had been no communication among personnel in IT, legal, records management, or business management about the case and what, if anything, should be done from an information management perspective.

Seemingly, nobody in this case completely understood his/her information management role. Nobody understood the role of those around him or her, or how each person's role was interdependent. The company learned, albeit too late, that it was failing in IMC. Cases just like this happen every day in organizations just like yours.

The Information Management Compliance Battle

Organizations today are caught in a battle—a battle with new rules and growing stakes. A battle for which few have been sufficiently trained and for which new weapons are still being invented.

It is a battle between the way we did things yesterday and the way that the courts, regulators, boards, shareholders, customers, employees, and partners expect us to do things today.

A battle between emerging technology tools and burgeoning compliance criteria.

A battle between today's path of least resistance and tomorrow's compliance failure.

What is Information Management Compliance?

Information Management Compliance (IMC) is an approach to information management that is designed to help organizations manage information in a way that meets legal, regulatory, business, and operational goals. IMC is a simple framework based on core principles from the legal and regulatory worlds that can be applied to virtually any activity in an organization that involves the creation, receipt, or use of information.

IMC has seven key elements:

1) Good policies and procedures

2) Executive-level program responsibility

3) Proper delegation of program roles and components

4) Program dissemination, communication, and training

5) Auditing and monitoring to measure program compliance

6) Effective and consistent program enforcement

7) Continuous program improvement

These elements of IMC are explored in detail in *Information Nation: Seven Keys to Information Management Compliance,* Randolph A. Kahn ESQ. and Barclay T. Blair, AIIM 2004.

This is the Information Management Compliance (IMC) battle.

Whether through direct experience or through exposure to the plethora of high-profile news stories, court cases, and regulatory investigations over the past five years, everyone in business today should be aware that the rules for information management have changed. Businesses face a new reality of compliance challenges related to retaining, preserving, finding, producing, using, and controlling their information assets.

Organizations are trying to adapt to these new realities. In a recent survey, 80% of respondents stated that they had recently made, or soon planned to make, significant changes to the way that they manage information.[1] As illustrated in the pie chart on page 7, they are making profound changes in organizational structures, new technologies, audits, training, and new policies. Such changes represent a significant departure from the way that information has previously been managed within most organizations.

But are these changes happening quickly enough? Despite their best efforts, many organizations continue to struggle with IMC. Less than one-third of those surveyed believe that they have made significant progress in updating and adapting their information management programs. A mere 13% had deployed an enterprise-wide approach to managing content.

In the midst of such upheaval, organizations today require individuals who are armed with a comprehensive understanding of information management and its attendant IT, legal, business, and records management challenges. Individuals are needed who can guide the organization and help it make informed decisions on policy, purchasing, and system configuration across the information management landscape.

In short, organizations today need Information Nation Warriors.

Planning to Make Major IMC Changes
(as a percentage of respondents)

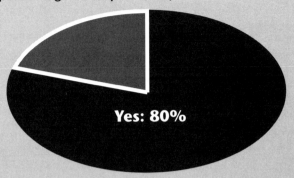

Yes: 80%

Source: *Information Management Compliance: 2004 Progress Report*
Kahn Consulting, Inc., August 2004

www.kahnconsultinginc.com   ©2004 Kahn Consulting, Inc.

Top 5 Factors Driving Industry-Wide Change in IMC Practices

1) Issues discovered through compliance auditing and monitoring

2) A regulatory action or penalty

3) Failure to find information needed for a lawsuit, audit, or investigation

4) A lawsuit or court action

5) A security breach

Source: *Information Management Compliance: 2004 Progress Report*
Kahn Consulting, Inc., August 2004

www.kahnconsultinginc.com   ©2004 Kahn Consulting, Inc.

Top 5 IMC Changes Planned or Already Made

1) Create new policies/update existing policies

2) Conduct employee training

3) Conduct information management audits and assessments

4) Make a technology purchase

5) Change organizational structure

Source: *Information Management Compliance: 2004 Progress Report*
Kahn Consulting, Inc., August 2004

www.kahnconsultinginc.com   ©2004 Kahn Consulting, Inc.

The Information Nation
Warrior Quadrants

Information Nation Warriors are people like you—
people who share responsibility for some aspect of an
information management program's development or administration. Warriors have different backgrounds, educations,
and roles within an organization, but each is in a unique
position to help the organization address its IMC challenges.

Today's IMC battle is complex and is only becoming more
complicated as more business is done electronically, as
technologies grow in sophistication, as information volume
grows exponentially, and as laws and regulations demand
greater accountability and transparency. Winning the IMC
battle, like any battle, requires the right combination of
planning, intelligence, skill, resources, and management.

Information Nation Warriors play a crucial role in this battle, and must understand:

- Their role and responsibilities
- The role and responsibilities of other Warriors through-
  out the organization
- How their skills and expertise can help, and where and
  when they need the expertise of others
- How to ask the right questions
- Where to go for answers
- How to communicate both needs and solutions

A key concept of Information Management Compliance is
proper delegation. It is the responsibility of executive
management to properly delegate information management compliance roles. The success of an information
management compliance program depends upon its implementation and administration by individuals with the
right mandate and the right training. This is often easier

Which of the following events are real?

• Due to storage limitations, the U.S. government's computer systems delete huge volumes of terror-related intelligence information before it has even been translated or reviewed.

• A federal agency is ordered to disconnect its computer systems from the Internet due to inadequate network security that would allow a hacker to alter, delete, or move original government records.

• The developer of a popular instant messaging application advises users that vulnerabilities in the product could expose computers running the software to security risks, potentially allowing remote access to the computer's contents, even when no chat session was taking place.

• A government litigant estimates spending in excess of $2.5 billion for a large class action suit—just to search for potentially relevant information pertaining to the case.

• U.S. election officials rely upon the sales representatives of electronic voting machine vendors to tell them whether or not election results are accurate, because the computer code running the machines is a proprietary trade secret that cannot be evaluated by an independent third party.

If you answered "all of them," congratulations—you are correct. As amazing as these scenarios seem, each is real and demonstrates the profound, ongoing gap between what is required in information management and what today's organizations actually do.

said than done, especially in large organizations that must juggle divergent and rapidly changing corporate cultures, technology infrastructure, and legal and regulatory requirements. Today's reality is that information management is multidisciplinary. It requires the expertise and participation of individuals with a wide variety of backgrounds.

At a minimum, today's Information Nation Warriors need to be grounded in four fundamental areas, or Quadrants, of IMC expertise.

The Quadrants are not intended to make an IT professional into an attorney, for example, but rather to help an IT professional understand legal issues central to IMC; to help an attorney understand what makes IT tick; or to help a records manager align her program with business goals. In other words, to help Warriors, regardless of their background, to arm themselves with a well-rounded understanding of the IMC battle.

I. Information Technology Quadrant

Information technology has become central to the way that we do business. As a result, today we create digital information of greater volume and value than ever before—information that must be controlled and managed.

Can you be a critical technology purchaser so that your organization gets the functionality it needs today, without having to wait for the "pie in the sky" capabilities that may come in the next version of hardware or software development? Are you tracking the evolving information management technologies as they become available and can you make recommendations to the company about how to invest resources to achieve the greatest impact possible?

As an IT Warrior, you must:
- Take Control of IT Today [Chapter 4]
- Bridge the Gap Between Policy and IT Management [Chapter 5]
- Be Prepared for Problems [Chapter 6]
- Build Compliant IT Systems [Chapter 7]
- Apply Best Practices and Standards [Chapter 8]
- Be a Critical Purchaser [Chapter 9]
- Use Project Management Expertise for IMC Success [Chapter 10]
- Understand Your IT Organization [Chapter 11]

II. Legal Quadrant

An increasing number of laws and regulations have an impact on the way that information must be managed and it is important that the legal fundamentals of IMC are understood by more than the organization's attorneys. Failure to consider the legal implications can result in project failure—or worse, liability in all sorts of varieties and sizes.

Have company retention rules been updated to address recent changes in the law? Can you access the necessary information and make it available in a few short days if required to do so by a state regulator? Given that your company does business in all 50 states, do you know what each state's laws say about storing information electronically? Do you understand the burden that "technologically neutral" laws place on you to do the right thing? Do you understand the legal implications to the technologies you purchase, considering that even the best technology improperly implemented or managed may create a legal liability?

As a Legal Warrior, you must:

- Translate Law into IT Reality [Chapter 12]
- Address Legal Issues throughout the Information Lifecycle [Chapter 13]
- Assess Your Electronic Discovery Readiness [Chapter 14]
- Ensure That Legal Responsibilities Are Clear—Especially When Trouble Strikes [Chapter 15]
- Make Informed IMC Legal Decisions [Chapter 16]
- Don't Try to Buy Compliance [Chapter 17]
- Strive for IMC Consistency [Chapter 18]
- You May Not Like It, But You Still Need to Comply [Chapter 19]

III. Business Quadrant

A critical challenge of IMC is finding and building support for the program. By learning how to think like an executive and how to speak the language of business, the Warrior can help ensure that the IMC program addresses the organization's business as well as compliance goals. Failing to align your IMC project with business drivers may mean failure for the entire initiative.

Can you link the IMC initiative to one or more strategic objectives of the organization? Do you know who in management will champion the IMC cause? Do you have a change management plan to address the people issues of implementation?

As a Business Warrior, you must:

- Make the Business Case for IMC [Chapter 20]
- Use Business Management Techniques for IMC Success [Chapter 21]
- Find an Executive Champion [Chapter 22]
- Learn to Articulate the Business Value Of IMC [Chapter 23]
- Manage Change [Chapter 24]
- Align IMC with Business Goals [Chapter 25]
- Run IMC Like a Business [Chapter 26]
- Build and Manage the IMC Team [Chapter 27]

IV. Records Management Quadrant

IMC must be built on a foundation of records management (RM) expertise. Determining what must be retained and for how long is a central function of RM that must be brought into the IMC world.

Can you distinguish information from records, and are you able to provide guidance to the organization's workforce to make sure they are retaining the right stuff? Is RM working with IT to help manage the vast quantities of e-data that may not resemble a record but may nonetheless need to be managed according to company retention rules? Have you developed simple retention rules that can be applied on the fly, given the new e-world in which every employee is now ostensibly a "records manager"?

As an RM Warrior, you must:

- Make Value Judgments About Information [Chapter 28]

- Address the New Records Management Reality [Chapter 29]

- Simplify Records Management Rules—Even Though Technology May Be Complex [Chapter 30]

- Put a Face on Records Management [Chapter 31]

- Teach Your Organization That All Employees Share Records Management Responsibilities [Chapter 32]

- Use Records Management Expertise to Aid Business Continuance [Chapter 33]

- Harness Technology to Manage E-Records [Chapter 34]

- Don't Forget Records Management Fundamentals in the Digital World [Chapter 35]

Assessing Your Information Nation Warrior Quotient

Are you the Information Nation Warrior your organization needs?

Answer the following self-assessment questionnaire to determine your Information Nation Warrior Quotient (WQ). The inability to answer "yes" to the five questions in each quadrant should signal the need to bolster your WQ.

I. IT Quadrant

- If you had to justify an IMC software purchase on the basis of ROI or TCO, could you?

- Do you understand the priorities of the IT department and how they will impact your IMC projects?

- Do you have a liaison in the IT department that advises you about new electronic business processes as they come online so that you can help address any record keeping issues that arise?

- Would you be able to tell the IT department what functional requirements you would need in an IMC application?

- Do you know the extent to which the IT department has configured systems using audit trails and log files, and why this is important?

II. Legal Quadrant

- Do you know the difference between information, records, and evidence?

- Do you know which regulators have an interest in how your organization manages its information?

- Do you know how to structure a click wrap agreement properly to increase the chances a court will conclude it is a valid contract?

- Do you understand the IMC implications of Sarbanes-Oxley?

- Do you know what the courts are saying about the responsibilities of organizations and their counsel relative to notifying employees of an active Legal Hold?

III. Business Quadrant

- Do you know the CEO's top 5 priorities for the coming fiscal year?

- Have you met with a senior executive to discuss how your IMC efforts will address the coming year's business goals?

- Is there any IMC project you are working on that adds profit to the company's bottom line, and if so, has its potential impact been conveyed to management?

- Given 30 seconds, could you describe the value of IMC to a business executive?

- Do you have an executive "champion" that understands IMC and supports your efforts?

IV. Records Management Quadrant

- Do you know if your organization's retention rules consider legal requirements and legal considerations?

- Would you be able to develop a plan for applying the organization's records policies and retention rules to records stored on employee desktops and laptop computers?

- Do you know how to develop an electronic communications retention directive and who you need to work with in the IT and Legal departments to get it done?

- Are you able to create retention rules that are simple but still thorough and consistent enough to allow employees throughout the company to apply the rules on an ongoing basis?

- Do you know how the organization's information systems have been designed to support electronic records policies and procedures?

warriorquadrant I

Information Technology Quadrant

Take Control of IT Today

Information technology (IT) is no longer just about automating business processes. IT is the way that business is done today. As a result, IT management must be about more than just making sure that systems function properly or are available when we need them. Today, IT management strategies must also include legal, regulatory, record keeping, and other IMC considerations.

For example, consider the challenges that an email system administrator traditionally faced:

- Number of system users
- System capacity
- System uptime
- Mailbox size, attachment size
- Email server patches
- System throughput

Compare this to the new challenges that today's email administrator (or *someone else* within the organization) must address—in addition to the challenges above:

- Control and ownership of content
- Acceptable email use policies
- Email privacy
- Spam and virus control
- Laws and regulations specific to email messages
- Accessibility for electronic discovery
- Enforcing Legal Holds by preventing purposeful or inadvertent deletion
- Retention and storage of records

Even by looking at only one of the many information systems that organizations rely on today to run their businesses, it is clear that the realities of IT management have changed. Simply put, if organizations do not take control of their IT, it will take control of them—in the form of unmanaged business content, compliance risks, and costs. In that regard, does IT work with RM to understand how those "tired" retention rules can help IT manage all sorts of databases, systems, and business applications?

The growing acceptance of digital information for legal purposes has cleared away many hurdles concerning how this information can be used, but in some ways the freedom to do business electronically only seems to compound the problem. How do we process, manage, and retain all this digital "stuff" in a way that serves and protects our business and legal interests?

As organizations take action to control and manage IT with compliance in mind, Warriors both inside and outside of the IT department increasingly need to play a role in providing guidance on the IMC implications of IT.

Where Warriors Need to Be Involved

IMC is not a consideration in every decision made in IT. However, there is little doubt that IT is becoming increasingly regulated and that courts and auditors are becoming increasingly sophisticated when they examine IT decisions made by an organization. As a result, Warriors need to be involved throughout the IT management process, including:

1) **Evaluation.** Look for technology that has been built with IMC in mind, and does not simply pay lip service to compliance considerations in marketing literature. Clearly define your information problem and compliance requirements so you will be better able to determine whether a vendor's product passes muster.

2) **Acquisition.** The Warrior should participate in purchasing decisions that impact IMC. Service Level Agreements

and other aspects of the purchasing cycle can have a major impact on an organization's ability to respond quickly to a court or regulator's demand for electronic records from a hosted application.

3) **Configuration.** Software and hardware must be configured to meet the unique demands of the organization and its business and technical needs. Configuration decisions, such as those involving access controls, error checking, and audit trails can have a major impact on IMC and should be evaluated by the Warrior.

4) **Management.** The ongoing management of IT is critical to IMC. The IT administrator must ensure that the latest security patches are applied to servers, confidential information parked on a shared drive is not available to those not authorized to see it, and access to company information is revoked when an employee leaves the organization or relevant workgroup.

5) **Decommissioning.** Retiring outdated systems and migrating data to new systems provides multiple opportunities for mistakes, including the introduction of errors or material alteration into data, inadequately purging old systems of records still requiring retention, or exposing company trade secrets to outsiders when computers are donated to the local community college. IMC issues must be addressed throughout the entire IT lifecycle.

Benefits of Spam?

The fight against spam may actually help improve the authenticity of electronic records. How? Through the development of technology designed to authenticate email senders. Various Internet Service Providers and email providers are combining forces to come up with a standard solution to fight mail "spoofing," or the sending of email under false sender names. Given the volume of business transactions in which email plays a key role, the ability to have greater certainty about the identity of email senders could be a key benefit that comes from such initiatives.

With IT vendors knocking at the door with new hardware and software solutions almost daily, organizations must evaluate an endless array of IT to find what suits their needs.

Purchasing, implementation, configuration, and management decisions must be driven by IMC policies and procedures—not the other way around. In other words, IT should never be purchased in an IMC vacuum. Rather, IMC issues should be part of the criteria used when these decisions are made. This only makes sense—as we increase our reliance on IT systems, we also increase our reliance on the output of those systems. And, unless we manage IT with IMC needs in mind, the information generated by IT may become a liability rather than an asset.

Before technology is purchased and implemented, there must be an articulated legitimate business benefit for the technology and adequate company controls and directives to address issues that will likely arise. Problems arise when management allows the advocate of a given technology to sell them on new solutions without fully analyzing the IMC implications.

Warriors need to get involved and provide guidance when IT decisions that will impact IMC are being made. Talk to the employees that will be using the IT systems to find out how their use of the tools could have IMC implications. Question a broad sampling of your organization, including company lawyers and records managers. Getting legal guidance upfront can save your organization a lot of inconvenience, hassle, and money in the long run. Discussing RM needs can identify what new content will be created, whether it is a record requiring retention, and if so, where and how it should be retained.

In our consulting practices we recently received a call from a Chief Compliance Officer asking for advice on a product selection while the IT executive and the vendor company's salesperson were present in his office. Times have changed in lots of ways and what you buy now likely will have ongoing RM, business, and legal implications, so consider them upfront.

Consider the following real-life scenarios where organizations failed to establish IMC policy or to adequately consider IMC issues related to IT use and management:

- Realizing that many employees are using instant messaging anyway, the IT department provides a link on the corporate Intranet to a site where employees can download a free instant messaging client. Two months later it is discovered that the software has a major security hole, and company trade secrets have been exposed.

- A company purchases a tape backup system, which comes with a "suggested" backup policy that routinely recycles previously filled tapes back into the system to be overwritten and reused. The IT department implements the vendor's policy without any consultation with legal or records management. However, the company is involved in litigation and the backup tapes contain database information legally required to be preserved and produced. The company is severely sanctioned for allowing the information to be destroyed.

- Several employees establish weblogs or "blogs" on the corporate Intranet, which can be accessed by thousands of employees worldwide. One of the bloggers, a top salesperson, uses his blog to describe a recent sales department retreat held for top salespeople at a Las Vegas strip club. The blog is used as a key piece of evidence in a lawsuit from a former employee alleging sexual discrimination.

- A marketing associate working on a direct mail campaign is about to miss a key deadline, so she decides to post the company's list of customers on a "hidden" webpage so the mailing house can download it, instead of physically delivering it on CD. In the heat of the campaign, she forgets to remove the information from the Web server; it is indexed by a popular search engine, and shows up in the search results whenever a search is run on the company's name. Several of the customers sue, and the company's reputation is devastated.

There's no question that mobile devices make us more productive. They might allow us to work on that long commute home or provide a lifeline to the office for last minute questions or necessary information.

With more employees than ever before staying connected and working outside the office, the most heavily fortified internal systems can be undone by poor management of mobile computing. Consider the following scenarios:

- You're going to Reno to give a presentation on a new product rollout, but in your rush to catch the plane, you leave your laptop in the backseat of the cab. Your presentation, along with other confidential documents and the company's current encryption key, are on the hard drive.

- Your company provides a service that offers cell phone users the option of receiving individually tailored advertising in the form of a text message. You're reaching thousands of receptive customers, but one of them decides to sue a vendor you represent for false advertising. How are you going to prove which message got to his phone, or even be sure he saw it?

- An office romance goes sour and looks like it may turn into a sexual harassment claim. The parties involved are sending nasty-grams back and forth over portable devices.

- You sit down in the coffee hut and use your wireless-enabled PDA to upload customer lists to your laptop. A curious college student a few tables away is browsing network traffic with a packet sniffer he downloaded off the Net. How secure are your devices?

These scenarios and many like them can and do happen regularly, but the benefits of mobility are so overwhelming that organizations tend to overlook the risks.

Failing to manage your information assets outside the office can result in:

- Inability to retain needed business records, communications, and transactions created or stored on portable devices

- Inadequate controls on the creation or alteration of records, allowing access to anyone that gets their hands on the mobile device

- Inconsistency in adhering to the company's Records Management policy that ultimately undermines its legitimacy

To effectively minimize these risks, the Warrior must consistently and adequately address **all** of the company's technology. Be as specific as you can in spelling out responsibilities for retaining and protecting data on portable devices. You may need to create a specific, understandable, and practical set of rules for each type of portable device your road warriors use.

Bridge the Gap between Policy and IT Management

Organizations today face new expectations from courts, lawmakers, auditors, regulators, and a host of other parties about the way that technology is used and managed. The Warrior's challenge is to help the organization to not only understand these new expectations, but also to help the organization practically address their impact on the way that information is managed.

The realities of today's new era of IMC have made concepts like "internal controls," usually associated with the financial auditing industry, applicable to the IT world. Internal controls are an important concept for the Warrior to understand and apply, and are a valuable tool for bridging the gap between IMC policy and IT management.

What Are Internal Controls?

A process designed . . . to provide reasonable assurance regarding the reliability of financial reporting and the preparation of financial statements . . . and includes those policies and procedures that . . . [p]ertain to the maintenance of records that in reasonable detail accurately and fairly reflect the transactions and dispositions of the assets of the registrant; [and] [p]rovide reasonable assurance that transactions are recorded as necessary to permit preparation of financial statements in accordance with generally accepted accounting principles. . . [2]

Sarbanes-Oxley Definition of "Internal
Controls Over Financial Reporting"

How Important are Internal Controls?

Months before the 2004 U.S. presidential election and the continuing concerns regarding the integrity of voting equipment, there was a similar problem in the 2004 presidential recall referendum in Venezuela. Even before the Venezuela election was held, there were allegations from the opposition (who went on to lose the election) that the vote and the future results could not be trusted because the electronic voting equipment (which ironically was manufactured in Florida, the location of the 2000 U.S. presidential voting machine scandal) could not be trusted. Imagine spending millions on technology and millions more to roll it out, only to have it undermined before it is even used or a real-life problem has been detected.

This definition of internal controls comes from the accounting domain. In this world, an internal control might include, for example, a requirement that any company check over $10,000 remitted to a vendor must be signed by three company directors. This internal control is designed to prevent fraud and ensure that money is properly spent.

The real advantage of internal controls is brought home in the context of an audit. When the company is audited, the auditor does not have to manually review thousands of company checks to see if they were properly signed. Rather, she can look for evidence that the controls were documented and employees were properly trained on the requirement, and she can take a sample of checks in order to ensure that the internal control was properly implemented.

The IT world also uses internal controls. For example, it is common for IT to establish a policy that all employees must have a unique username and password before they can have network access. A CIO reporting on security within his organization could point to such a policy, along with IT staff training and system information, to demonstrate that each employee has a unique username and password, eliminating the auditor's need to manually check each entry.

Other examples of IT controls that support IMC include:

- Patch management and application updating procedures
- Procedures for monitoring the health and performance of critical applications and systems
- Emergency response plans for disasters and security breaches designed to minimize damage and loss and reestablish functionality
- Independent certification of the qualifications of IT staff that manage critical systems and handle sensitive data

IMC and Internal Controls

The Sarbanes-Oxley Act (SOX), which generally applies to public companies that are listed on a U.S. stock exchange, requires companies to regularly report on the internal controls they have established to ensure that their financial reporting is accurate and reliable.

While SOX is focused on financial information, it is clear that the internal controls contemplated by the law impact much more than just accounting systems and financial information. In fact, SOX emphasizes the importance of ensuring that the records **underlying** financial reports are trustworthy. In today's organizations, which rely on IT throughout every aspect of their business, ensuring trustworthy records cannot happen unless IT is configuring and managing its systems in a way that supports this goal.

From enterprise databases and billing systems to departmental caches of contracts and HR information, there are dozens if not hundreds of IT systems in today's organizations that create and house information that may be material to a company's financial reporting. Each of these systems must be managed and controlled in a way that the organization (and outside parties such as courts and regulators) can have confidence in the information from those systems.

IT controls must address not only the need to ensure that systems are reliable and functioning properly, but also that they are protected from unauthorized access, alteration, and destruction. In addition, such IT controls must extend to the full range of systems that contain material information, which increasingly includes corporate messaging systems.

Internal controls can be a valuable ally in helping the Warrior tackle this challenge—whether the Warrior is inside a company that is mandated to employ internal controls by law, or inside a company that simply wants to get a grasp on the IMC challenge.

Internal Control Frameworks

COBIT Framework (Control Objectives for Information and Related Technology)

The COBIT Framework,[3] first released in 1996, initially gained attention as a guide to successfully aligning and managing IT with business needs, with a focus on reliability, security, and operational effectiveness. Today, COBIT is increasingly viewed as a framework for helping organizations comply with SOX and meet additional IMC challenges.

The COBIT Framework is an IT governance model that provides over 300 control objectives addressing topics ranging from the way that IT departments are managed to the configuration and monitoring of software applications. For example, COBIT outlines a high-level control objective of "managing data," which is designed to ensure that *"data remains complete, accurate, and valid during its input, update and storage."* This objective takes into consideration issues such as document controls, data administration policies, data backup and recovery, and legal and regulatory requirements.

COBIT and similar IT controls frameworks provide important guidance to the Warrior on a method to take control of IT and manage it in a way that will support IMC goals.

COSO Framework (Committee of Sponsoring Organizations of the Treadway Commission)

The COSO Framework, published by a voluntary private sector organization, provides a much broader internal control framework than COBIT. The focus of COSO is on internal controls designed to support business, operational, financial, and compliance goals. It is a "generic" framework in that it is designed to be applicable to organizations of all sizes in all industry sectors.

COSO identifies several areas that have both a direct and implied impact on the IT department. For example, COSO recommends that:

- A mechanism (e.g., an information technology steering committee) [be] in place for identifying emerging information needs.
- A long-range information technology plan [be] developed and linked with strategic initiatives.
- Sufficient resources (managers, analysts, and programmers with the requisite technical abilities) are provided as needed to develop new or enhanced information systems.[4]

Warriors should familiarize themselves with the concept of internal controls and investigate the way that frameworks like COBIT and COSO can help them bridge the gap between information management policies that support IMC and the way that IT is managed and controlled.

Be Prepared for Problems

One of the most common mistakes made by organizations today is a failure to prepare for the day that their IT systems, and their management of them, will be scrutinized by a court, regulator, investigator, auditor, or another outside party. These parties may poke, probe, prod, and examine each and every aspect of IT management at your organization, and may spend hours questioning IT staff and others with knowledge about IT at the company.

The Warrior's role is to help their organization prepare for the worst. To prepare, for example, for that day—which will come—when electronic records, documents, and other evidence will need to be unearthed, preserved, and produced.

Get Your IT House in Order

> "My concern was that if I was ever asked to produce these thousands of backup tapes, regardless of what they concerned—they did not just contain mail, they contained everything—that it would be a task that would be beyond the human endurance to try to figure out what was on those things."
>
> Rambus, Inc. v. Infineon[5]

When the subpoena arrives or the regulator comes knocking, it might be too late to get your IT house in order. In electronic discovery, requests for information may come with very tight turnaround times. Unless systems have been structured in a way that promotes quick location and access of information, complying may be difficult or impossible. In some cases, regulators may expect an email message, for example, to be produced within a few hours or days. An organization was recently fined $10 million by the SEC, because, among other things, they "failed in a timely manner to produce electronic mail, including a particular mail exchange . . ."[6]

So, the Warrior should prepare now. Compiling a basic inventory of the organization's computing resources may make a big difference. The following types of information may make the "search and produce" process far less painful:

1) The physical location of the technology or system (address, building, floor, room number, etc)

2) The name of the technology or system

3) The model number

4) The manufacturer

5) The current operating system and its version number

6) Any other current versions of software needed to use or retrieve records, and their respective model numbers

7) The name of the employee who "owns" the technology or system and the mail address and telephone number for him/her

Data Today, Evidence Tomorrow

To be readily accessible for electronic discovery or perhaps more importantly for routine business operational purposes, data must be properly indexed and retrievable on demand. Indiscriminately retaining all of your organization's email, for example by dumping it onto backup tapes, can drastically increase the cost and time involved in retrieving discoverable

What Needs to Be Preserved?

Which of the following need to be preserved when a lawsuit is filed?

1. All relevant documents

2. All potentially relevant records

3. All relevant voice mail messages

4. All potentially relevant information

5. 2 & 4 above

6. All of the above

If you answered number 6, "all of the above," you are right. In fact, today anything potentially relevant no matter what it looks like or what it is—even various drafts, non-records, or temporary messages—may need to be preserved and potentially produced.

Preparing for Litigation: A Checklist

Know what the law requires in terms of e-records preservation:
The law dealing with discovery may vary from state to state, so tailor preservation efforts accordingly.

Decide who needs to be notified, and what they need to be told:
Provide specific instructions to all employees on what needs to be preserved and how to go about it. Notification may need to extend to contractors, outsourced storage providers, and other parties that have responsive information. Remember: the law requires that litigants to a lawsuit produce potentially relevant information in their "care, custody, or control"; which means that if you have a contract with another firm to manage your information or manage a business process, you likely have to produce to your adversary the information in their control as well.

All forms of information and tangible objects are included:
All recorded information, regardless of media format, and all tangible objects related to the matter must be preserved.

Take immediate action: Do not wait for a subpoena or formal notification to take action. Suspend disposition efforts immediately when litigation, audits, or investigations can be reasonably anticipated or contemplated.

Create and manage documentation: Formal written policies and procedures must be in place to outline the preservation process.

It's not just about destruction: The law prohibits alteration, mutilation, concealment, covering up, and falsifying evidence. Maintain proprietary software and encryption keys necessary for the retrieval of records data.[7]

material while making irrelevant yet potentially embarrassing messages available for review.

Do you have a process in place for classifying data so that, at a minimum, company records are retained and "junk" with no ongoing value is disposed of? The proper classification of information is not only necessary to help your organization prepare for electronic discovery, but also to help your business run more effectively and efficiently.

At a minimum, data classification practices should identify and address:

- Data needed for regulatory compliance
- Data potentially relevant to pending or ongoing litigation, audits, and investigations, including information that might normally not be retained by an organization
- Data required for running day-to-day business operations and managing the business now and into the future

What is a "Record" Anyway?

There is currently no definition of "record" that is universally used by all organizations, and for good reason. Definitions serve the community that they are created by and each community has different needs. The key characteristic of a good "record" definition for your purposes is that it is broad enough to encompass all the information you need to retain for business, operational, legal, regulatory, or historical purposes, without being so broad that employees cannot understand or apply it in practice.

The following definition of "record" encompasses key records concepts and is the one that we often use in our consulting practice:

A record is information recorded on a tangible medium (paper or electronic media being two common examples) and intentionally retained and managed as evidence of an organization's activities, events, or transactions because of its business, operational, legal, regulatory, or historical value.

Courts and regulators don't care about the definition of records or non-records, data, or "significant business information" when they are involved. Whatever exists that is even potentially relevant needs to continue to exist in a complete, unaltered state, even if it did not need to exist in the first instance, until the matter is resolved. In the context of a lawsuit, the records, non-records, or anything else that is potentially relevant would be produced as part of a "document" production. That's why having rules and following them is keenly important. In fact, there are two sets of needed rules: 1) records policies and retention schedules used during regular business environments, and 2) different rules that supersede and suspend the routine retention rules in the context of threatened, imminent, or filed lawsuits, audits, or investigations.

- Data essential for business continuance and disaster recovery, including business, financial, and operational
- Data with security, confidentiality, and privacy considerations, such as company trade secrets and customer data

Just because you refer to electronic stuff as data or information does not mean that is not really a company record. If data or information has ongoing business, legal, compliance, operational, or historical value, then it probably is a company record and should be managed accordingly.

Data in Hiding

Data is generated from a broad array of devices and comes in a variety of forms, so it's little wonder that some important information is able to slip under the radar. Interactive Voice Response (IVR) for instance, allows users to interact with database systems using a touchtone phone for activities such as order entry or the review of account information. If an employee uses IVR services to amend his investment portfolio by phone, how is the transaction memorialized? Accurate records of touch-tone selections may be necessary to prove, for example, that it was an employee input error instead of system error or a malicious employee with access to the system that caused the problem. Metadata—hidden data that provides information about the record (data about the data)—is another example of record information that can potentially be overlooked. Mail headers contain important evidentiary information related to origin, authorship, and routing of the message. Word-processed documents and spreadsheets in digital form contain authorship information and formulas unavailable in their printed counterparts. Courts may require the digital versions of these records in spite of paper reproduction for these very reasons.[8]

Detailed psychological records containing the innermost secrets of at least 62 children and teenagers were accidentally posted on the University of Montana Web site last week in one of the most glaring violations of privacy over the Internet . . . unlike a medical file left open on a counter in a doctor's office, these electronic medical records, once placed on the Internet, were exposed to a potentially vast audience.

Los Angeles Times[9]

Protecting content covers a broad range of security and privacy concerns. There are several potential problem areas that should be addressed in policy and be revisited on a regular basis:

Incident Response: A response plan should be in place to determine if problems are being caused by a hacker or internal illegal activity. Forensic analysis can be used to determine the nature and origin of the threat, if data has been affected or removed, and where to focus efforts to improve data security.

Patch Management: Software must be consistently updated with the latest security patches and fixes to maintain system stability and prevent intrusion or contamination by malicious code.

Disaster Recovery: Vital records must be backed up and moved off-site to assure continuance of business operations in the event of a disaster. Plans must be updated on a consistent basis, taking into account new risks and complications.

Misappropriation of Information: Policy and software safeguards must be in place to prevent employee misuse of information. Policy must clearly state that all records are company property that must be returned when employees leave the organization. IT must have the ability to lock down computer access and track employee actions to prevent misconduct.

Customer and Employee Privacy: Privacy violations hurt customer relations and can land your company in court. Personal information must be maintained as outlined in the company's privacy policy, while protected information, such as credit card data and medical records, must be secured in compliance with applicable laws and regulations.

Confidential Information: All employees must know what information is considered confidential and should treat it as such. Confidential information sent via email should be labeled as such in the message header. Secure encryption should be used to transmit confidential information outside the company firewall.

Data Corruption: Important data should be backed up in multiple locations, mirrored, or striped across multiple drives for redundancy in order to prevent loss due to corruption.

Build Compliant IT Systems

7

Part of the Warrior's challenge is to think in new ways about existing problems. This can be particularly challenging in the world of IMC, which requires Warriors to draw from their IT, legal, business, and records management base of knowledge when making decisions and providing guidance.

It is especially true in the IT world, where many ideas about "the way things are done" must be challenged if IT systems are going to be built and managed in a way that meets compliance requirements.

For example, most developers and designers have not been taught to consider the compliance implications of the user interface ("UI") and system architecture decisions they make. As a result, many software applications and online services that in fact have serious legal implications have been developed without their architects having access to the information that is needed to protect their organizations from serious legal risks and liability.

Where an application or online service has legal importance, such as one that uses electronic signatures, the risks of a poorly-designed UI or system architecture extend far beyond frustrated users and a deluge of help desk requests. Poor design can lead to expensive litigation, severe penalties from government regulators, and negative media coverage that can diminish a company's value and prevent it from achieving its business goals.

Vanity Plates and System Design Disaster

Bad system design often has unintended consequences that can be disastrous—and also sometimes just plain funny. A practical joker in Delaware recently applied for—and was issued—a vanity license plate for his motorcycle that read "NOTAG."

Soon after, our intrepid funny man began receiving hundreds of parking tickets in the mail. The reason?

The transportation department's computers had stored a backlog of traffic violations that had been committed by vehicles that had no license plate—in other words vehicles that had "notag."

Of course, once the system realized that it now had a name and address for the backlog of violations committed by the NOTAG scofflaw, it automatically issued the tickets.

System Trustworthiness and Record Trustworthiness

A basic principle of information system design is that *content* should be separated from its *presentation*. The benefit of this approach is flexibility—data can be viewed, processed, and presented in multiple forms for different applications. The IT conception of what is right or good is diametrically opposed to the records management conception of a record, which requires the unity of the content, structure, and context.

But the "content" of an electronic record is much more than mere data. In fact, such "content" may be needed to meet requirements for completeness, accuracy, integrity, and reliability. As such, applying the "content and presentation separation" principle to electronic records may severely minimize their legal effectiveness and thus create unnecessary risk.

Assume, for example, that electronic records from a Web application used for purchasing books online are created in the following way. The data relating to the transaction (i.e., book title, shipping address, etc.) is collected and managed in a database. Then, when the transaction is completed, the data for the transaction is combined into a table that is "printed" as a digital Portable Document Format ("PDF") file. The PDF file is then emailed to the customer and is deleted from the production system.

In this hypothetical case, the company is relying upon the database as the ultimate source of transaction records for "official" purposes, as they have kept no instance of the **actual** record as it was delivered to the customer. In other words, although the customer received a record that included **content and presentation,** the company has only retained a record of the **content**.

Is the content enough for legal purposes? Although there are many ways to create electronic records, federal and state laws, regulations, and industry guidelines provide many requirements and principles for the creation and retention of electronic records. System architects, and those who manage the information generated by such systems, should consider the concepts below when making design and configuration decisions.

Record Completeness

If you use a standard electronic form that is populated by the database information, can you prove which form field referred to which database entry?

For example, does the number "225" printed from a database table by itself demonstrate that this number was the purchase price, a birth date (February 25), weight, or some other figure?

If not, what other information will be required to prove the meaning of this number, and can that information be managed and delivered in a reliable and complete way over time?

Can you prove that the standard form template that is populated by the database and delivered in its complete "content and presentation" format to the customer has not changed since the customer received it? What about **three years** from now?

A client recently sought guidance on a related issue. If his company relies on numerous database-centric systems like their ERP, CRM and billing applications that are constantly changing, how will they prove to an auditor or a regulator in the context of a Sarbanes-Oxley related inquiry what the quarterly database record looked like or stated? After all, unless they capture the database at the precise moment in time as a distinct record, the next time a transaction is entered into the system everything changes.

Record Format

Is the record you deliver or make available to the customer capable of being viewed, printed, stored, and accessed over the long term in a complete and accurate form?

Can you prove over the long term exactly what the customer received, including the electronic record's physical appearance, the size of the fonts, and the interrelationship of the various textual and graphical elements of the record? In a real-life example, a financial services company provided a "clear and conspicuous privacy policy" in red, type 24 font in the electronic Web version, but retained only the content, which was all black and only type 12 font size, just like all the rest of the content. Arguably the retained record was no longer "clear and conspicuous" according to the regulation.

Can you prove these things regarding the record that the company retains if you had to in the context of a legal dispute?

Record Integrity

Can the system be used to prove that transaction information **has not been altered** in the database after the complete "content and presentation" record was delivered to the customer?

The building of IT systems and the creation and management of electronic records are a clear example where the Warrior must play a key role. The Warrior can help system develop-

Challenging Electronic Records: Real-life examples

People v. Superior Court[11]—Computer forensics used to discover that the defendant had falsely created "backdated" letters and billing statements was introduced as evidence in the trial.

Campbell v. General Dynamics Gov't Sys. Corp.[12]—The court ruled that a mass email to employees containing links to an employment policy did not constitute sufficient notice about the policy, so the policy did not apply.

AFD Fund v. United States[13]—Testimony from a company witness about the use and management of the company's databases was essential to the admissibility of electronic billing records as evidence.

State v. Voorheis[14]—Text of instant messages found on the defendant's computers was admissible.

ers understand the idea that the most intuitive, efficient, or "correct" approach to IT architecture is not necessarily the approach that will meet compliance requirements. The consequences of failing to address business or technological goals in system design are well-understood and taught. However, the consequences of failing to address compliance requirements are rarely well-understood and rarely taught. It is the responsibility of Warriors from across the company to understand and address each other's concerns while working together to create an application that meets business goals and protects the company's interests.

Attacking Electronic Business Processes

When an organization seeks to use electronic evidence to tell its side of the story in a legal dispute, there are many ways that attorneys can attack the authenticity and reliability of that evidence.

- Attacking the way the system was managed, including who had access to the system and when.

- Attacking the process that created or managed the electronic record to show some other action was desired.

- Attacking the record to show it doesn't reliably prove the facts purported.

- Attacking the design to prove the user of the system didn't understand the implications of the action taken.

To withstand such attacks, system design, configuration, and maintenance decisions must be made with IMC requirements in mind.

Don't Reinvent the Wheel: Best Practices and Standards

Many of the problems the Warrior will face when dealing with IMC are new, and there may not be a body of ready-made solutions to draw upon. At the same time, many organizations, institutions, and individuals are working on solving the same IMC problems that the Warrior faces. The Warrior should seek out best practices, industry standards, and the good work done by others and incorporate it. It does not make sense to reinvent the wheel. The IT world has long benefited from a body of best practices that help to establish the policy and procedural foundation.

Best practices are fundamental to IT and should be in IMC as well, for the following reasons:

1) Can provide concrete guidance on what is considered reasonable and prudent and provide real direction on what your organization could or should be doing.

2) Applying industry standards can help to increase your organization's credibility in the industry.

3) Following best practice may make you and your organization more comfortable that the action you are taking is what others similarly situated would take.

4) Best practices memorialize your efforts to "do the right thing," showing good faith or reasonable actions.

5) Best practices can be tailored to the needs of your organization—pick from the best and ignore the rest.

6) If best practices work well for others in your industry, they will likely work well for you.

7) Why expend efforts coming up with original methods when you can stand on the collective shoulders of giants?

Best practices are quasi-standards that have been identified as accepted methods for achieving specific business functions, goals, or industry requirements. Organizations should seek the most effective way to operate, apply, and test various processes internally, then judge the value of these processes relative to their goals. Once a process is recognized as a best practice it may continue to develop organically, acting as a catalyst for new best practices or being co-opted to meet the needs of other organizations to the extent they find it useful—moving to other departments, businesses, or industries.

Industry Standards and the Law: An Example

For purposes of determining whether an e-record is admissible, the Canada Evidence Act provides that evidence regarding adherence to a standard in the creation of records and the management of e-records system may be introduced.[15] An example of such a standard that may be useful is the National Standard of Canada, CAN/CGSB-72.11-93, *Microfilm and Electronic Images as Documentary Evidence,* first published by the Canadian General Standards Board (CGSB) in 1993 and amended in 2000.

The Benefits of Best Practices and Standards

Applying tried and true methods to business functions and processes makes sense if your organization is looking for quick and solid results while eliminating the guesswork. But there's more to be gained in following the footsteps of successful organizations than might be apparent at first.

The most compelling reason to consider best practices is because "experts" have focused time and resources on an issue for which you have limited perspective. It seems both reasonable and prudent to "borrow" the collective knowledge embodied in the best practice for your own use. From an IMC perspective, adhering to industry best practices and standards can send a clear message that you are serious about managing information in a compliant way—which can be helpful if your organization's actions are ever challenged by a regulator or in the context of a lawsuit. While not a shield from liability, certification against an industry standard, or adoption of a standard as part of your "standard operating procedure" (SOP) may be viewed as inherently reasonable, which can have a significant and positive impact on a court or regulator.

Following best practices can also save your organization money by eliminating much of the guesswork involved in carving out policies and procedures. They serve as a guidepost to what works, and more importantly what doesn't. Taking the time and energy to concoct homegrown solutions through trial and error for any process when a solution already exists may be costly and imprudent.

The good thing about best practices is that they tend not to be overly rigid methodologies, but concepts that continue to develop and mature over time. Organizations are not required to adhere to best practices, but should use them as a compass to help point your organization in the right direction. Learn from these industry standards; apply what works best for your organization and its specific needs. Starting from this solid foundation you can add to your industry's body of knowledge by continuing to refine what already works—making for better business industry wide.

Keep in mind, however, that the pace of business, legal, and technological change is increasing rapidly. The best practices of today will likely not be the best practices of tomorrow, and ad hoc "standards" continually pop up as the result of case law. It's up to the Warrior to keep abreast of new developments and anticipate changes on the horizon.

Industry standards and best practices relevant to IMC come from a variety of sources, and Warriors should seek out those sources that are appropriate to their industry and issues.

When researching best practices and standards, Warriors should keep the following issues in mind.

- **Look to case law.** While case law is not a "best practice" in the typical sense of the word and may only apply to the litigants in the specific court, there are useful principles that nonetheless can be extracted from court decisions. Many legal issues in IMC continue to evolve regarding digital evidence, electronic records and signatures, privacy, liability for security breaches, electronic discovery, and a whole host of other issues as they are decided by the courts. Warriors should work with their legal department to ensure that such developments are researched and tracked as part of IMC efforts, such as policy drafting. In one recent example, the court in *Zubulake v. UBS Warburg*[16] has issued at least five separate rulings on a variety of issues around electronic discovery. The most recent ruling involved the court's exploration of what should be expected of a company in notifying its employees of the need to preserve relevant information for the pending lawsuit. What the court determined is that more proactive communication was needed and that the company should be more proactive on an ongoing basis to ensure that employees are doing the right thing. The way the ruling impacts our consulting practice is that the new court created "best practices" that might be useful to adhere to. Since the time of the ruling we have already incorporated the court's "suggestions" into guidance provided to clients. While not a perfect defense, if your company ever ends up defending the issue, you can always tell the court that you followed the legal "best practice" of the day.

- **Look for examples rather than templates.** Although policy templates can be a useful tool for getting a sense of the kind of issues that IMC policies could address, avoid the temptation to rely on stock templates. Fleshed out examples of actual policies are much more useful to give you a sense of how a particular organization in a particular industry dealt with particular IMC issues. Examples may be harder to come by, but are not impossible to find. Online legal research sources are useful, as are industry groups for information management professionals, which promote sharing of such information. Government and public universities are two good sources of information, as they often will post their policies on their website. But remember that your policies will probably need to be different from these examples, because you will likely have a different legal landscape to live within.

Best Practices: Real World Examples

There are probably dozens, if not hundreds of potential sources of best practices that are potentially useful for Warriors. Warriors should seek out sources that best reflect their business, technological, and legal realities and requirements.

Here are some examples of the type of IMC guidance you can expect to find within best practices documentation:

ISO 15489, Information and documentation-Records Management. This ISO standard on record keeping provides guidance on "[t]he standardization of records management policies and procedures," and is designed to ensure "that appropriate attention and protection is given to all records . . ."

Forensic Examination of Digital Evidence: Department of Justice.[17] Best practices for examining digital evidence state that examiners should gain "access to all password-protected, encrypted, and compressed files, which may indicate an attempt to conceal the data from unauthorized users. A password itself may be as relevant as the contents of the file."

IT Controls: COBIT.[18] This framework for managing information technology and information states that a best practice for handling data is that the "conversion of data is tested between its origin and destination to confirm that it is complete, accurate and valid."

American Bar Association. The American Bar Association has changed its Discovery Standards to better deal with discovery of e-information. At the ABA's 2004 annual meeting, members adopted amendments to the ABA's Civil Discovery Standards addressing issues related to the discovery of electronic documents to deal with new issues confounding litigants and courts alike. The amendments are not "law" but provide lawyers guidance as a "best practice" to deal with e-discovery issues.

Electronic Discovery: The Sedona Principles.[19] This set of best practices for electronic discovery states that organizations "should adopt policies that provide rational and defensible guidelines on the treatment of electronic documents. These guidelines should be created after considering the business, regulatory, and tax needs of the organization, including the need to conserve electronic storage space on e-mail and other servers."

Be a Critical Purchaser

Large scale purchasing of hardware and software can be intimidating, involving huge dollar amounts and often complex processes that require a great deal of attention to minute detail. Compounding matters, for a variety of reasons not the least of which is complexity, enterprise IT implementation often results in failure. While complex technology implementations can be of huge value offering great benefits, they can also be expensive and high-risk ventures. According to a recent study, nearly half of software projects are completed over budget, 90% are completed late, and 60% are considered failures by those who initiated them.[20]

The purchasing of software and hardware designed to help an organization with IMC is no different. Identifying, capturing, retaining, and managing the massive volumes of information created in today's organizations is a complex exercise that puts great demands on the hardware and software used for this task.

The Warrior can play a key role in helping the organization make the right decision when it comes to purchasing software and hardware tools. There are two basic scenarios where the Warrior's IMC knowledge should play a key role in this process. First, the Warrior should help the organization when any technology is purchased that has IMC implications. Second, the Warrior must play a central role in the evaluation, purchasing, and implementation of IT specifically designed to help with IMC. In both cases, the Warrior can learn from the techniques and strategies used by IT departments in making IT purchasing decisions.

There are many types of software and hardware throughout an organization that either indirectly impact IMC or are directly used in the management of information. The Warrior should strive to ensure that where IT has an IMC impact, the Warrior has a voice in the purchasing process. Given the complexity of IMC, input from Warriors with legal, RM and business backgrounds will be useful as part of the purchasing process. Think holistically and collaborate holistically.

Although there are many ways to categorize IT systems, Warriors can use the following basic breakdown to help them understand and anticipate IMC issues in the technology purchasing process.

- **Infrastructure:** The so-called "plumbing" of the organization's IT operation, infrastructure includes the servers, routers, wires, and other components that form the core of an organization's IT architecture. Servers used for shared network storage are a simple example of an infrastructure component. Infrastructure can be very complex in large organizations. End users typically are not directly exposed to an organization's IT infrastructure—no more than they are exposed to the wires and junction boxes that carry electricity throughout a building.

  Infrastructure choices can have major IMC implications. For example, the type of storage system used to store and archive email can affect an organization's ability to respond to a regulator's request to retrieve a specific message on demand, and can affect the trustworthiness of the stored information.

- **Business applications:** Software applications (and their related hardware) that support business processes such as Accounting, Enterprise Resource Planning, Customer Relationship Management, and Sales Force Management are examples of business application categories. End users typically have little control over the configuration or administration of such applications, but they are the primary creators of the information used and stored in these systems.

The records created and stored in such applications are typically the "lifeblood" of an organization—the information that would be required for business continuance in the event of a disaster. The information contained in these applications is often referred to as "structured" content in that it is created and stored in a structured database.

- **Desktop applications:** Software deployed to the user's desktop, or other individual user devices, supports a variety of functions across the enterprise, including word processing, spreadsheets, and various communication tools.

These applications offer unique management challenges, as they are difficult or impossible to manage centrally—as is the information they generate. And the desktop has become increasingly mobile with the use of laptops, PDAs, and wireless devices—all of which are even more difficult to manage and control.

Information created in desktop applications is usually defined as "unstructured information"—text-oriented information such as email and word-processing documents that reflect the ad hoc, unstructured way that human beings tend to work, communicate, and think.

- **Management tools:** Some software applications, such as Document Management or Records Management, are not used to create information, but rather to manage what was created in other applications. Software used to classify and retain email messages, index and search records, and provide version control are examples of management tools.

Management tools are often employed to help organizations manage "unstructured" information by storing it as documents in a structured system. They can also be used to manage the "output" from a structured database application, such as a financial report or an invoice.

- **Utilities:** This broad category includes applications that don't necessarily serve a specific business function, but may nonetheless be central to an organization's back-office operations. Encryption, file compression, and server management tools fit into this category.

Utility applications can be quite complex to implement and have IMC implications. Like desktop applications, the management of utilities can be challenging since they are often deployed to the desktop and usage is not centrally controlled.

In the IT community, cost justification most commonly uses one of two models: Total Cost of Ownership (TCO) or Return on Investment (ROI). The projects most likely to get funded are those that make the best economic case for the outlay of capital and implementation expenses. Using TCO or ROI will likely be the difference between moving forward and having your project rejected or put on indefinite hold.

Total Cost of Ownership (TCO)

TCO is a model developed by an IT analyst firm in the 1980s to help organizations understand the **total cost** of IT purchases. The key to TCO is understanding that the total cost of an IT purchase comes from both *direct* and *indirect* costs. So, when purchasing a desktop computer, for example, organizations need to consider not only the cost of the hardware, but also indirect or "soft" costs such as:

- Help desk employee costs
- Hardware upgrades and installation labor costs
- Electricity
- Cost of downtime
- Depreciation

Warriors must learn to understand and calculate both direct and indirect costs in the IMC world.

Return on Investment (ROI)

By viewing an IT purchase in much the same way as one would a financial investment, ROI is a model designed to help organizations understand and calculate the financial upside (or downside) of an IT purchase. Although ROI calculations can be very complex, at its most basic level, ROI is a calculation of the total cost of an IT purchase against the total return of the purchase, over time.

As with TCO, determining indirect costs and benefits is part science and part art. For example, although "improved employee morale" might be a benefit of purchasing a system that makes it easer for employees to find the information they need, it is challenging to financially quantify this benefit. One approach is to focus on what is measurable, such as surveying a statistical sample of employees to find out just how much faster they find information on average, and calculating the financial benefit based on the time saved multiplied by salary costs.

Total Cost of Failure (TCF)

In some cases, models like TCO and ROI may not be sufficient to quantify the benefit of IT purchases designed to improve IMC. Warriors should look to the Total Cost of Failure (TCF) model to help them build their case.

Whereas TCO is about calculating the economics of taking action, TCF is about calculating the economics of failing to take action, or of taking the wrong actions. As with calculating TCO, calculating TCF is not a science, and requires organizations to make educated guesses about possible cost sources in the future, the likelihood of particular cost sources occurring, the dollar amounts attached to various cost sources, and other factors. The costs associated with IMC failure can come from many direct and indirect sources. In order for a TCF estimate to be valuable, it must include consideration of the full range of possible costs.

By taking even a brief look at one aspect of Information Management—electronic discovery—it becomes clear the sources of TCF cost are varied and can add up very quickly. What is the potential Total Cost of Failure for not having an adequate base of technology and policies to respond to the requests of the courts, regulators, auditors, and other parties for electronic records and other information?

- **Search and retrieval costs.** In the past, courts have required organizations to search through massive volumes of email, at great cost, to find information responsive to litigation.

- **New software.** Organizations may be required to buy special software or even develop their own software that will allow their data to be searched, compiled, copied, and/or translated into a different format.

- **Penalties for destruction of evidence.** The courts take destruction of evidence very seriously, and as we have seen throughout this book, criminal and civil litigation can result.

- **Employee time lost to participating in e-discovery efforts**. This "soft cost" can in fact be the source of greatest expense, as dozens of IT and other staff are tied up in the discovery effort.

- **Forensic experts** for data recovery and testimony.

- **Technology experts** for custom coding.

- **Computers,** servers, and networks taken offline, or made unavailable.

Warriors can find additional information about applying the TCF model in *Information Nation.*

The Request for Proposal

The Warrior should seek to examine any application that is being considered for purchase by their organization for relevant IMC implications. One of the ways that the Warrior can accomplish this is by becoming involved in the drafting of a Request for Proposal (RFP), a formalized mechanism for eliciting vendor information.

RFPs are used in the IT world to specify the system requirements the purchaser is looking for and invite vendors to respond to these requirements in a proscribed way.

RFPs can be a powerful tool for two reasons. First, for the obvious reason that they clearly communicate to vendors what you are looking for. Second, for the less obvious reason that they force the purchasing organization to sit down and figure out in detail exactly what they want. This process can be very valuable to find out what various groups feel the real needs are, reveal problems with preconceived notions about the nature of the problem the organization faces, and establish a foundation for measuring the success of an implementation.

The Warrior should play a key role in the development of RFPs and in the evaluation of responses where the IT system being considered has IMC implications. Keep the following considerations in mind:

Inhouse or Outsource?

The choice of whether to use internal or outside resources to meet your application needs depends on your organization's culture, resources, and the type of application.

Managing software using internal resources can be advantageous in that business needs and system infrastructure may be better understood and hopefully better utilized. Upfront costs for deploying the system using this approach may be greater than the method described below, but may be less costly over time.

Using an outside vendor to "own" the problem for you can reduce manpower and equipment costs by eliminating the burden of maintaining the system. This approach can be used for data storage or for an entire system application. Companies doing the outsourcing are commonly referred to as Application Service Providers (ASPs) or Storage Service Providers (SSPs). Whether this approach is more or less costly varies based on the companies involved and the applications supported.

When evaluating these approaches, Warriors must consider the IMC implications of each choice. Having company information assets on company computers in company facilities is of great importance to certain individuals and companies. An internal application may provide more control over compliance-related design and configuration issues, but outsourced applications may already be built to comply with best practices and industry standards.

If your organization outsources, remember to negotiate what happens when the relationship ends (they always do at some point) or if the company goes out of business. Your company information is tied to their computers and software so negotiate access to technology once the contract is terminated, address ownership issues and access rights, and make sure to get their written agreement that no matter what happens the outsourcer will not hold your information hostage.

- **Be realistic:** Don't ask for a nirvana-type application that does not exist or would require expensive customization. Do your industry research.

- **Leave room for alternative input:** Vendors—who live every day in the universe you are describing in your RFP— may have a different perspective or valuable insight into your problem that you have not considered. Leave room in the RFP process for vendors to suggest alternative solutions or approaches.

- **Ask for specific answers:** Although your problem, from the vendor's perspective, may look exactly like the problem they have seen at dozens of customers, do not accept stock responses where it really matters. Work hard to identify where and how your problem is different from what others in the industry are facing, and articulate your unique needs in the RFP.

- **Push for commitments and precise clarifications:** If marketing material makes claims about possessing the needed functionality, make sure you pursue answers to understand precisely what their technology does and does not do.

Choosing the Right Vendor

Once you've developed an RFP that clearly defines your system requirements, you can get serious about choosing a specific package or product.

Don't limit yourself to evaluating only the big name suppliers that come to mind. In your initial research, find as many alternative solutions as possible and begin to whittle your choices down from there. Many segments of the IMC market are in their early stages.

If you need more information about which vendors provide the needed service or product, you can contact a technology analyst research firm that does ongoing research and can provide (usually for a fee) a list of vendors by technology categories. Professional and trade organizations often have directories of vendors in their areas of interest.

Look for vendors that:

1) Specialize or have experience in your particular industry and regulatory environment

2) Offer products that meet your business requirements but don't tack on expensive unnecessary features

3) Have a solid financial foundation

4) Have a strong customer support and customer satisfaction record

5) Are ahead of the innovation curve and focus considerable efforts on R&D

6) Offer solutions (and pricing models) that are scalable and flexible enough to support future growth

Pilot Projects

A pilot project is a small rollout of an application over a set time period that allows you to evaluate the vendor's solution on a small scale and decide whether the system is worth a large long-term investment. Pilot projects allow you to see if the product can live up to the vendor's claims in the real-world setting of your particular environment and culture. Pilots may take much of the guesswork out of the final implementation plan because the buyer doesn't have to rely solely on projections that may not apply to the organization's specific circumstances.

Given the choice of an outright sale of their technology and a pilot project, you should expect that most vendors will try to avoid involvement in a pilot project. If, however, your organization is going after a large-scale implementation, running a pilot can have huge benefits and should be seriously considered.

Why Bother with a Pilot?

Ontario's Ministry of Community and Social Services set out to implement a new welfare system—"a real time, Web-enabled application that embedded some 800 rules governing social services payment eligibility, [created to] prevent fraud, reduce caseloads and improve service." Initial estimates pegged the cost at $135 million. Seven years and $214 million dollars later, the province is attacking the system as inefficient and difficult to use, requiring upgrades which will cost taxpayers millions more.[21]

Use Project Management for IMC Success

The National Archives and Records Administration's (NARA) project to electronically archive government records recently came under fire from the Government Accountability Office.[22] The GAO found that NARA's methods used to track the program's cost and schedule were inadequate, which could result in cost overruns, quality issues, or inability to meet the required deadline. NARA is the nation's official records keeper. If the experts can't get it right, what does that mean for the rest of us?

Project management tools, techniques, and expertise have long played a central role in the way that IT does things—from creating software to implementing complex IT systems. Warriors need to learn from IT, and leverage their project management expertise to help make IMC initiatives a success.

Project Management Documentation

IMC projects, like any other complex project, will not be successful without a lot of prep work. Program goals and parameters must be crystal clear to the project team, sponsors, customers, and other stakeholders. A good deal of time should be spent talking with stakeholders in the project.

Such stakeholders might include:

- **End users:** Employees and contractors using the IT system who will actually have to comply with IMC policies

- **Business units:** Representatives from each business unit who can identify the unique challenges in their operating environments that must be considered

- **Project sponsors:** Those who are funding the project

- **Key administrative areas:** Representatives from Finance, Accounting, Human Resources, Compliance, and other areas as appropriate

- **Other Warriors:** Representatives from IT, Legal, Business, and Records Management departments

The fundamentals of project management demand that project requirements, timelines, and responsible groups or individuals are captured and documented before the project begins.

Warriors should strive to create the following project management documentation as part of any IMC project:

- **Work Breakdown Structure (WBS):** The WBS lists the tasks required to complete the project and the estimated resources needed to complete each task. Use the WBS to set up your schedule and to present cost estimates to your sponsors.

- **Gantt charts:** A Gantt chart is one way to visually represent the various tasks within a project, illustrating the resources and time required to complete each task, dependencies amongst tasks and resources, and task start and end dates. Simple Gantt charts can be created using spreadsheets and there are several dedicated project management products that can create them for more complex projects. The figure on page 67 shows an example of a Gantt chart for the creation of email retention guidelines.

- **Requirements:** This document outlines specifically what the project must achieve in order to be successful. Having the requirements down on paper and "signed off" by project sponsors is important to prevent the project from slowly spiraling out of control due to scope creep—demands for little "add ins" that will equal big headaches when taken together.

- **Closing documentation:** Throughout the project, track your progress, the challenges you faced, and how you dealt with obstacles for future reference. What worked and what didn't? Each project adds to a body of knowledge that will make future undertakings easier to manage. Record the details of each project to establish best practices and lessons learned.

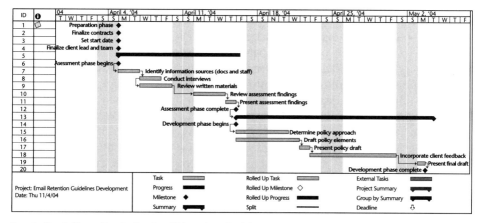

Sample Gantt Chart: Developing Email Retention Guidelines

© 2005 Randolph A. Kahn and Barclay T. Blair

Managing Resources

The primary purpose of organizing any project is the management of resources—people, money, and time.

- **People:** Make sure you get the right people with the right skills and the right attitude. Don't just fill seats. Team members are going to have to "own" the project to make it a success.

- **Budget:** Be careful when calculating cost estimates. Since you want to keep costs below the stated estimate, include a "contingency allowance" to account for unforeseen expenses and avoid cost overruns. If available, use project management software to "load" the project, helping you consider costs that have a tendency to be overlooked. To maintain your budget, keep to your project schedule. To stay on schedule, avoid scope creep.

- **Schedule:** Set up your schedule to track dependencies—tasks that must be completed before the next phase of the project can begin. Delays in dependent tasks can create a bottleneck, leaving team members sitting around waiting for completion of the dependent task so they can start their own work. Don't underestimate the time required to complete each task on the way to the goal. Make sure you requisition equipment and supplies early enough so that waiting for them doesn't hold up the project. Stick to your schedule; the most common cause of cost overruns is lack of schedule management.

Project Management Certification

Earning certification in Project Management can be extremely useful for implementing larger projects but may be overkill unless project management is a major ongoing job responsibility. Start learning PM skills through reading and Internet research, and gain practical experience by getting actively involved in ongoing projects. As you refine your skills, you'll be better equipped to decide whether or not a certification is right for you and your organization.[23]

Managing Scope

Your venture is not really a project unless it has a definite beginning and end. If it goes way over budget or misses the deadline, management is going to start viewing it as a money pit. The surest way to miss your deadline is to become a victim of scope creep—adding in "little extras" not agreed upon at the outset. The requesters will argue that adding a little tweak here and there isn't going to be a big deal. Too many little tweaks, however, are going to cause complications that could easily set you back or even cause the project to fail.

Warriors must manage the scope of a project by having everyone's expectations clearly stated on paper at the front end, describing what needs to be done, the resources allotted to do it, and the deadline for completion. Requested add-ins can be captured for a future upgrade project.

Communication

Communication plays a major role in facilitating change. As change begins to unfold, it will affect only a small percentage of the organization, but will then spread out to affect more and more employees as the project progresses. As you might imagine, this is the perfect environment for developing rumors and negative or uninformed opinions. Keeping everyone in the organization involved at some level will help prevent a negative reaction to the change, which may adversely affect project outcomes.

Change management best practice is to inform employees of:

• How the change affects them, especially the benefits

• Why the change is important to the organization

• Where they can get their questions answered

Being available to answer employee questions and generally interact with them concerning change issues will decrease resistance. Involving staff members will give them a stake in the project, rather than engendering feelings that it's just another waste of time imposed from above by persons far removed from "the real work."

Understand Your IT Organization

A key part of the Warrior's role includes working with the IT organization. So it is critical that the Warrior understands how IT "works," how it fits within the enterprise, and how the culture of IT is determined. Even for Warriors who sit inside the IT department, it is useful to step back and look at the IT big picture.

Views of IT

IT plays many different roles in different organizations, and the way that IT departments are structured and managed varies widely across industries. The way that IT is viewed in your organization can have a major impact on the role that IT plays in IMC.

There are many different ways to view the role of IT, but for the Warrior, it is useful to understand two of most common perspectives on IT:

- **Tactical view:** In this view, IT fulfills a tactical, service-oriented role. IT is there as a kind of service bureau, primarily focused on supporting the business as required and keeping computer systems operational. Organizations with this view of IT might look favorably at outsourcing their entire IT department to another company, as they do not view IT as central to what they do, and consider IT somewhat as a commodity. IT is there to "keep the lights on."

- **Strategic view:** In this view, IT is seen as a value-generating organization that performs activities that are central to the competitive advantage and ongoing success of the organization. IT is more likely to lead initiatives independently and to be more closely aligned with the business. These IT departments are also more likely to develop applications internally (even to the point of licensing their "products" to other business units or outside the company), and may take a dim view of outsourced services or hosted applications.

The purpose of identifying these views is not to point out that one is right and one is wrong, but rather to help Warriors think about how the perception of IT within their organization will impact their IMC projects.

Test Your Warrior Quotient:

Which of the following is generally NOT considered in the typical IT project?

1. Software needs

2. Hardware needs

3. Records Management implications

4. Business needs

5. Legal requirements

If you answered numbers 3 & 5, you would be correct. When building the functional specifications for an IT project, it's usually the technical and business issues that are addressed. Very seldom are the RM and Legal needs and requirements seriously considered—two essential elements for success.

Consider that every time a computer is added to a business process, there will be information output of some kind that is generated. Your challenge is to determine how to manage that output and whether or not it constitutes a record. Increasingly the IT world is being legislated by rules, laws, or regulations; whether these are security or privacy concerns, business issues, or preservation requirements, it's critical to carefully consider the implications of what you plan to do.

Assessing Your IT Department

The type of IT department that you have within your organization depends on a number of factors, including your industry, company culture and history, resources, and leadership.

Consider the following questions when assessing the role the IT department plays in your organization:

- Does your IT department focus primarily on tactical needs or does it actively participate in your organization's strategic initiatives?

- How well does IT align with your organization's strategic needs? Does your organization allow IT to dictate processes and strategy, or does it find the right fit that allows technology to further business goals?

- Does your IT organization understand how its tactical functions can affect strategic needs (positively and negatively)?

- How solid are your organization's business plans regarding IT implementation? Is IT often blamed for failures that could be the result of poor strategy or a misunderstanding of what IT solutions are capable of?

The Impact on IMC

Whether your IT department is viewed tactically or strategically can affect the way that IMC projects develop and move forward.

The Tactical View: Pros and Cons	
Pro	**Con**
More willing to consider off-the-shelf information management solutions, which may shorten implementation cycles	Less willing to invest in new or cutting edge information management tools
More willing to get support for involving outside resources to specifically assist in IMC projects	Less funding available for approaches to IMC that rely heavily on IT investment
May be less emphasis on economically justifying IT purchases and development in applications that are well-known	More difficult to build support for major IT investments

The Strategic View: Pros and Cons	
Pro	**Con**
More willing to build customized solutions that precisely meet your IMC needs	In-house development and implementation cycles may be longer than implementing off-the-shelf software
May find powerful IT sponsors for IMC projects that make project success more likely	Lack of interest from IT may doom IMC projects
May be more willing and able to perform complex integration work between information management applications, resulting in greater project success and lower costs	Unwillingness to bring in outside specialists may slow project implementation times

New Challenges for IT

The computer industry is already a multibillion dollar one and within the next generation will surely be America's largest. . .Yet research and months of interviews with government and industry representatives reveal little understanding of the growing impact of government regulation.

Government Regulation of
the Computer Industry, 1972[24]

Over thirty years ago, a study on government regulation of the computer industry concluded that there was little understanding of regulatory issues across the industry, even though there were a number of relevant legal developments. Today, the same study would likely find the same result—especially given the proliferation of laws, regulations, and court cases over the past thirty years that have a profound impact on the way IT is used and managed.

Aside from debates about whether IT's role is or should be tactical or strategic, like it or not, IT departments face a host of new challenges in the era of IMC. As discussed in Chapter 5, IT is increasingly regulated as a result of Sarbanes-Oxley and many other legal and regulatory developments.

IT departments need to strive to understand the impact of this newly regulated environment on what they do and how they do it. An increasing number of information and records management failures derive from inadequate investment in—and management of—information technology used for creating, retaining, and managing business records.

This trend is not likely to reverse itself as organizations' dependence on digital information continues to grow and email and other forms of digital information provide a growing target for litigators and regulators. Organizations must ensure that their deep reliance on information technology is matched by their commitment to ensuring that information in digital form is managed with at least the same care and attention as records in paper form.

Warriors within IT departments need to work to understand the other Warrior Quadrants so that they can help their departments step up and address these new challenges.

warriorquadrant II

Legal Quadrant

Translate Law
Into IT Reality

> . . . at the time that the Court entered the tempo-
> rary restraining order . . . directing that the Interior
> Department's computer systems be disconnected from
> the Internet, it had received evidence from a variety
> of sources indicating that the agency could not guar-
> antee that individual Indian trust data housed on the
> agency's computer systems was secure.
>
> Cobell v. Norton[25]

A U.S. House of Representatives subcommittee
recently found that Internet security was lacking at several
government agencies.[26] The Department of the Interior
(DOI) was singled out, however, due to an earlier court
mandate requiring them to secure Indian Trust assets con-
sisting of nearly $3 billion.[27]

In the lawsuit that followed, the courts called for tests on
the DOI systems by a computer expert, who proceeded to
successfully hack into the department's network, proving it
was insecure. As a result, the court required all DOI systems,
not just those housing individual Indian trust data, to be
disconnected from the Internet until it could be proven that
the network was secure.[28]

As this case demonstrates, the courts do not look kindly
upon organizations that merely pay lip service when it
comes to making legal requirements a technological reality,
even if it's the government that fails. Today there are hundreds, if not thousands, of different laws and regulations
that have an impact on the way that IT systems and the
information they house are stored, transmitted, retained,
used, managed, and disposed.

The challenge for Warriors is to help their organizations understand the impact of existing and emerging laws and regulations on IMC. This requires not only the tracking of developments in the legal world, but also a careful analysis of the business, technological, and records management implications of legal developments.

When translating laws into a technical reality, technology and legal professionals are going to have to work together to determine what the law or rule means and how to satisfy it. Some examples of what may be required include:

- **Satisfying the Letter of the Law.** Broad dictates within laws need to be interpreted, such as requirements that records are "secure," and systems promote "integrity" and "authenticity." IT Warriors must build technical controls into computing environments to satisfy the **letter** of the law. So for example, Warriors might have to translate into practice what a regulation means when it requires a system to "[v]erify automatically the quality and accuracy of the storage media recording process," as required by the SEC. Will read/write verification satisfy the rule? What is the quality of the recording process and how does it differ from accuracy of the recording process?

- **Satisfying the Spirit of the Law.** Regulations must be reasonably interpreted to meet not only the letter of the law but the **spirit** of the law as well. For example, how would you implement a regulation that states that a company must "store separately from the original, a duplicate copy of the record stored on any medium acceptable" (another SEC regulation)? The letter of the law would be satisfied by making mirror copies of hard drives and putting them on separate floors in the company home office. However, if the building goes down in a fire, would the spirit of the law, which seeks to protect the data against destruction, be satisfied? Clearly not. Sometimes you need to go beyond the literal words; the legal Warrior can help the IT Warrior make such translations.

- **Translating to solutions.** Take the plain meaning of a law and determine what proper technical solutions work, given the clear language. For example, the California Database Protection Act[29] requires that notice be provided to California residents if and when their protected private information is accessed by an unauthorized person unless the information is encrypted. How powerful an encryption software has to be used? What part of the record needs to be encrypted? Does all of the information need to encrypted, or just enough so that the recipient cannot determine whom the information relates to? The Warrior will have to make these judgment calls.

Compliance Failures Can Have a Major Impact

Letter from Tom Daschle, U.S. Senate, to Gale Norton, Secretary, U.S. Department of the Interior:

"It has come to my attention that numerous schools in my home state of South Dakota that are operated by the Bureau of Indian Affairs (BIA) recently lost their connection to the Internet. According to my constituents, this is a consequence of the recent court order requiring the Department of Interior to deactivate numerous websites and Internet connections as a result of lax security surrounding information about Indian trust accounts."

"I am extremely troubled by the fact that the court order to disable Internet connections in the Department of the Interior, the third of its kind since 2001, has caused a disruption in the Internet access at Indian schools in South Dakota, and across the country. Even more troubling is the fact that the students, faculty and administrators impacted by this disruption are in no way involved in the Cobell v. Norton lawsuit, which is the catalyst of the court order."[30]

> *Companies must have reasonable procedures in place to make sure that changes do not create new vulnerabilities. Just as consumers remodeling their homes would make sure that the doors still have locks, companies should make sure that sensitive data is still protected.*
>
> Director Howard Beales,
> FTC Bureau of Consumer Protection[31]

A large retail music outlet recently agreed to settle U.S. Federal Trade Commission (FTC) charges that a security flaw on its website placed its customer's personal information at risk. The settlement with the FTC required the company to improve security measures, by mandating website security audits every two years to be performed by third party security professionals.[32]

At issue were statements in the company's privacy policy that claimed user information was properly secured: "We use state-of-the-art technology to safeguard your personal information . . . you and only you have access to this information." The FTC asserted that the company's privacy claims were false and as a result violated the FTC Act.[33]

The FTC further alleged that the security flaw at issue was easy to prevent and fix, but that the company failed to implement effective controls and monitoring procedures to address its Internet applications, and failed to test its website security or properly train employees in this regard.

The lesson that Warriors can learn from this case is that good intentions—even if expressed in a great policy—are not enough. Policies and procedures are useful to help your organization express how it is going to comply with legal requirements, but they are only the first step. The reality is those legal requirements ultimately need to be translated into IT requirements—and that is a job that requires the involvement of Warriors with IT, legal, business, and records management expertise.

Warriors should keep the following in mind:

- IT should review IMC policies and report back on how they are going to make the policy into reality.

- Legal should review IMC policies and the plan on how the policy is going to be technically implemented, and provide feedback on their adequacy.

- Attorneys should ensure that IT and others are providing them with detailed enough information on how IT systems and procedures work so they can make an informed evaluation.

New Technologies, New Legal Considerations

> *"Better understanding and better tools are desperately needed if we are to take full advantage of the ever-increasing supply of information. . ."*
>
> UC Berkeley, "How Much Information."[34]

As technology evolves, so does the law—a reality that the Warrior must keep in mind when evaluating technology and its IMC implications.

For example, federal laws are changing to address law enforcement access to a new communications tool—Voice over Internet Protocol (VoIP). In the consumer market, VoIP enables users to make calls over the Internet, sidestepping long distance charges on traditional telephone use. VoIP use is also on the rise in business, and is expected to account for 75% of all voice traffic worldwide by 2007.[35]

The courts are wrestling with how to categorize VoIP. Is it a telephone network or an information service? In a recent case, a leading VoIP service provider attempted to block the Minnesota Public Utilities Commission from imposing the same laws on its services that apply to regulated telephone companies.[36] The court granted a permanent injunction in favor of the service provider, but legal changes regarding this new technology are still in the works.

Mel Cook, the head of the Business Communications Group calls a meeting to discuss requests by the employees to allow them to use Instant Messaging (IM). Which of the following issues should Warriors consider before allowing the technology?

- Does the technology create any information security issues that need to be addressed?

- Are instant messages considered a business record requiring retention and subject to being used as evidence in any formal proceeding?

- If retention is required, will the company technology be able to properly capture the various messages and the participants to the exchange?

- Will the capture of IM traffic violate wire tape laws in any states in which your company does business?

- Does any regulation require IM to be captured and managed?

If you answered "all of them," you are correct. All of these issues and many others should be considered and addressed before the decision is made to implement IM. For each new technology there will likely be legal, record keeping, and business issues that arise, which is why organizations increasingly need a band of Warriors to fight the battle.

Due to the portability and encryption capabilities of VoIP, the FBI is seeking new Internet eavesdropping rules (beyond existing wiretap laws) to access data traveling through broadband cable. This would potentially make all Internet Web traffic available to the FBI—email, instant messaging, and file sharing included.[37]

Such technical regulatory decisions have real business and legal implications. If VoIP is unregulated, how can organizations be properly protected from the actions of its new services provider? Who will protect the organization from viruses transmitted across the VoIP system that impact not only the organization but its customers as well? Will the system create recordings of calls and will there be phone records that may be needed for business purposes?

Warriors within organizations who are evaluating VoIP and other emerging technologies must carefully consider the legal implications **before** implementing the technology. Particularly when the technology and the law surrounding the technology are in their relative infancy, implementing the technology for sensitive and valuable business transactions may not be the best idea.

In our consulting practice, we spoke with a client who had completed a rollout of handheld devices throughout their entire sales force—thousands of employees. However, soon after the rollout, the company discovered that the handheld technology did not allow them to capture and retain information in the manner required by a key regulation. As a result, the handhelds were taken from the employees and the program scrapped—at a cost of millions of dollars—not to mention the "soft costs" of lowered employee morale and a broken sales process.

Warriors must help their organizations adapt to existing laws and prepare for future legal developments:

- **Get your house in order.** Ensure all systems comply with current laws and stay ahead of the curve when legal changes are in the works.

- **Consult with attorneys.** Lawyers who follow current case law will likely be the first ones to see changes on the horizon. Capitalize on their insight to adapt to developing requirements.

- **Consider legal implications before adopting new technologies.** Will adopting new IT solutions bring unforeseen headaches? Consider a full range of alternatives. New technology isn't always the best answer.

- **Keep one finger on the pulse.** Follow news of how laws are impacting organizations similar to your own and learn from their victories and mistakes.

- **Monitor IT at your organization.** Make sure you know what technologies are in use in your organization, and where and how they are being used. Do not allow IT to be used without legitimizing its use through policy.

Digital Rights Management (DRM)

DRM is the name for an emerging category of software tools to protect digital information from unauthorized access, use, or distribution. The market for this software is expected to grow from $36 million in 2003, to $274 million by 2008 (CNET news—Jupiter Research survey).

Initially focused on protecting commercial products such as music and movies, DRM is increasingly playing a role in protecting private company assets. But take care: the DRM software you purchase to protect your information could make it inaccessible in some instances. Giving employees the option to encrypt a given message and destroy the key used to access it is enough to give a records manager nightmares. Strict policy rules and effective procedures must be in place to ensure tools such as DRM software are consistent with the organization's IMC strategy.

In addition, remember that Section 802 of Sarbanes-Oxley prohibits the handling of evidence in a way that "alters, destroys, mutilates, conceals, covers up, falsifies . . ." it. Allowing employees to use encryption in such a way that prevents information from being found and decrypted could conceivably violate this requirement.

Address Legal Issues Throughout the Information Lifecycle

13

Do IMC legal issues and requirements in your organization become important only when the subpoena arrives in the mail, the regulator knocks on the door, or the lawsuit begins? Preserving and producing information in these situations is only one part of the information lifecycle that requires the Warrior's care and attention.

The Warrior must address legal issues throughout the entire lifecycle of the information management process. Warriors must guide their organizations on the way that information—and the systems that create and house that information—is managed from beginning to end. Each part of the information lifecycle contains unique challenges that the Warrior must address.

Creation and capture: Identifying, classifying, and collecting business content into the systems that will house and manage it.

Issues that the Warrior must address in this phase of the lifecycle include:

- Are there formal policies regarding how and when records are captured?

- Are there multiple parts of an electronic record that must be captured and managed?

- Is the record in a format acceptable to the court or regulator?

- Was the record captured in a trustworthy manner?

- Is the system that created and captured the record being properly managed?

- Have employees received training on creating professional business records? If so, has employee compliance been audited?

Records Creation: Timeliness Matters

An insurance company claims that a client violated his policy agreement by misrepresenting his medical history.[38] The company claimed the insured was a smoker, despite his indication on the company's insurance forms that he had not smoked in the previous twelve months.

The case required close examination of the insured's medical records. In one instance, the defense attacked the insured's inpatient medical record because of a "five-week gap between the time [the insured] was discharged from the hospital. . .and the date that [his physician] dictated and transcribed his discharge summary form." This, despite a hospital policy that required dictation within 48 hours.

The defense argued that the physician had "serviced over 600 patients during the interim period [and that] it was unlikely he would remember with exactitude what [the insured] had told him about his smoking a month before."[39]

The doctor's failure to create the record in a timely fashion—and in compliance with his employer's policy—called the credibility and reliability of the records into serious question.

Retain and Store: Efficient and accurate retention and storage of information in a manner that supports business and legal goals.

In some cases, content—particularly business records—may need to be preserved for long periods of time in a trustworthy and accurate manner, in which case organizations must make decisions about the most cost-effective and reliable medium and mechanism to use. Some industry regulators, such as in the securities industry, require firms to store electronic content in particular kinds of storage systems, often those that provide "write once, read many" (WORM) capability.

Examples of issues that the Warrior must address in this phase of the lifecycle include:

- How long must records be retained to satisfy legal and regulatory requirements?

- Are the records being stored in a way that prevents unauthorized access and alteration?

- Will the storage system and process likely be viewed as trustworthy by a court or regulator?

- Is there a migration plan to ensure that electronic records retained over a long term remain accessible?

Manage: Management of content to meet specific goals, such as improved customer service or compliance with retention requirements.

Examples of issues that the Warrior must address in this phase of the lifecycle include:

- Is private information accessible only by authorized parties?

- Are systems used to manage the information configured and managed in compliance with legal and regulatory requirements?

- When information is transmitted between systems or employees, is it adequately protected and managed?

Deliver: Providing timely and secure access to business content when it is needed to the systems and people who need it.

Examples of issues that the Warrior must address in this phase of the lifecycle include:

- Will information be produced in a timely manner to regulators and courts?

- What format for records production will the courts and regulators find acceptable?

- Will regulators and courts accept paper printouts of electronic information or must electronic records be produced in their original form? Is information stored on backup tapes acceptable?

Dispose: The final stage of the information lifecycle—information is discarded or destroyed.

Examples of issues that the Warrior must address in this phase of the lifecycle include:

- Have records been properly disposed of once their retention period is over, or is there a treasure trove of old records lying around?

- Is the digital information "really gone" from the disk drives on the computers we are about to resell?

- Are there any pending or ongoing lawsuits, investigations, audits, or other formal proceedings that require us to preserve this information beyond its retention period?

Manage "Unstructured Content"

Unstructured information is the free-form content that exists outside the confines of databases or systems, such as Enterprise Resources Planning systems and workflow applications, with fixed routines and pathways. This information, found in email messages, word processing documents, digital images, and PDF files, generally represents the vast majority of information in most organizations, with industry estimates placing it at 80% of all information that organizations create. This breakdown reflects the reality that business process are notoriously hard to define or "set in stone" because they reflect the way people work—in ad hoc groups that associate themselves around tasks and issues that are difficult to predict and control in an effective way.

In the past age of the mainframe and "dumb" terminal, information creation capability was more centralized and controlled. Businesses worldwide today use more than 300 million decentralized desktop computers that together have the capacity to store 150,000 terabytes of information.[40]

As a result, employees today have the ability to create (and destroy) massive volumes of content on their desktops. It is the Warrior's role to help organizations manage and control this content in accordance with legal requirements and business goals.

> *"Thus, the court has already found, as a matter of fact, that Rambus anticipated litigation when it instituted its document retention program."*
>
> Rambus v. Infineon[41]

A company holds a document shredding day, during which millions of documents are destroyed. The shredding is carried out according to the company's newly-minted document retention program, which spells out how and when documents may be disposed.

The trouble is, at the same time, the company is preparing for litigation. Company insiders later testify that they thought the reason they had the shredding day was to get rid of documents that might be discoverable in litigation. The company argues that it was just following its own policies and that disposition of the documents was necessary to help them deal with the vast volumes of data they had stored—not to thwart discovery.

The court is left to determine if the true intention of the document retention program was in fact to encourage and enable the destruction of evidence.

Although the ultimate outcome of this case is still being decided, its impact on the Warrior is clear. Like never before, courts today are closely examining how organizations manage their information—even to the extent of questioning the intent of IMC policies and procedures. This should be a wake-up call to the Warrior—the law today cares about information management—so the Warrior had better care about the law.

Which of the following could be a record?

• Voice mail

• The computer code representation from pressing a button on a
  telephone keypad

• Instant message chat

• Clicking on an action button on a website

• A computer log file

If you answered "all of them," you are right. In fact, all sorts of electronic content are rising to the level of being considered records. The problem is that
many forms and types of records today don't resemble the old paper records
that came before; therefore many electronic records are not being retained
properly, if they're retained at all.

Assess Your Electronic Discovery Readiness

The Warrior must play a key role in helping the organization understand and communicate legal requirements for information management. Nowhere is this truer than in the context of electronic discovery, when the organization must respond to lawsuits, audits, or investigations by preserving and producing information.

Electronic discovery is one of the greatest new IMC challenges that all organizations, large and small, in all industry sectors must face. The Warrior must be prepared to practically guide their organization through the electronic discovery minefield. The quiz in this chapter will help Warriors assess their ability to provide this guidance and identify areas that need improvement.

Assess Your Readiness

Answer True or False

(The correct answers follow immediately after the questions. No peeking!)

1) Playing "hide the record" and going into the "four corner stall" makes sense as a litigation tactic especially in the era of electronic discovery because there is so much to hide. Never agree with the opposing side on the scope or limitation of discovery, especially due to the ethical problems it creates.

Legal Holds Apply to Service Providers as Well as Employees

In a recent class action lawsuit against an insurance company, the defendant insurance company failed to preserve discoverable documents due to a lack of effective communication with third party service providers. Believing it would take too long to create a full backup of company systems, the defendant asked the service provider to image the organization's email server as of a specific date. The company, however, failed to provide them with a copy of the preservation order and counsel didn't speak with the service provider's employees or tell them to preserve all the company emails on backup tapes. The result? The service provider only took a snapshot of the server on the specific day requested and continued to overwrite backup email tapes, complying with retention guidelines but in violation of the letter and spirit of the law.[42]

Remember, just because you contract with a third party, does not mean you will not be held responsible for their failures. Generally, you won't be excused for failing to satisfy YOUR legal obligations because you hired contractors to help in the process and they failed.

2) As long as you have stored information—no matter where it is located or how accessible it is—your organization should be fine in responding to discovery requests. Remember, if all else fails, you can just give them the tapes or disks and let them worry about accessing the specific records.

3) Even if you make a paper copy of an e-record available to the opposing side, you may still need the electronic version and may have to give them access to the original, including access to your computing environment.

4) Once you have found all potentially relevant information, you have satisfied all your obligations to the courts. From that point on you don't have to worry about content integrity.

5) Finding and viewing responsive information today does not mean you will have continued access in the future due to changes in technology.

6) All you have to do is make a good faith attempt to find needed information. You can simply leave information where you found it, just be prepared to tell the court about your efforts.

7) A Legal Hold is really the same thing as following the organization's retention rules, so you should not need one if your Records Program is up to snuff.

The Answers

1) **False.** Putting aside whether or not such tactics and she-nanigans ever made sense, in today's reality it is clear that the risks outweigh the rewards. Today it is more appropriate to sit down early in the process with the opposing side to negotiate an agreement to limit the scope of discovery. Ample case law demonstrates that deliberate delay tactics can cost millions in penalties.

2) **False.** Making sure that needed digital information, documents, and records can be found and unearthed in a timely fashion may require the original software and hardware used in the creation and storage of the information. If you can't open and access the contents, don't expect the other side to be able to either. In one case, a court admonished a litigant for handing over thousands of tapes even though they knew the other side had neither the technical nor monetary resources to access them.

3) **True.** It is probably prudent to create an exact electronic duplicate of any and all responsive electronic information, documents, and records needed to be preserved or produced. Retaining and properly preserving the "original" electronic record in its unaltered form is essential. Further, it may be advisable to create a separate electronic archive for all responsive records needed for a particular case. Only records relevant to a particular matter should be viewable within the separated archive. By separating the responsive records you protect against irrelevant records being viewed by opposing counsel, if and when reviewed in their "native" format or system of origin, which could be allowed at the court's discretion. At a minimum, you should separate out records from other irrelevant or unresponsive information that are also stored within the same system or on the same media, so as not to inadvertently disclose non-relevant information.

4) **False.** Once records are determined to be potentially relevant to any investigation, audit, or lawsuit, take steps to protect those records from loss, destruction, or alteration. Consider protecting the information from inadvertent or intentional access using information security procedures and tools, such as access controls and encryption.

5) **True.** Long-term access will be bolstered by documenting where records can be found, produced, and printed several years from now. As part of your organization's litigation preparedness, it may be helpful to document what will be needed to ensure long-term access to the records as technology changes (i.e., new versions of software and hardware are implemented). With routine changes and upgrades to software and hardware, records created on older versions of software or hardware may not be accessible over time without continued access to the software and hardware used in the record's creation.

6) **False.** It may be useful to centrally manage records subject to production to bolster controls around the evidence and for quick and methodical retrieval later. Storing responsive records in multiple or unknown locations makes production more challenging and costly. Care should be taken with all responsive information to protect it from alteration. The process by which a responsive record is found and produced should be documented to the extent possible. It might even be prudent to document the electronic discovery process by creating a record to demonstrate what was searched, by whom, when, how, and so on.

   Such management evidence should show the efforts undertaken involving the record's retrieval, storage, re-creation, and production. It could also support the conclusion that all responsive records were found, preserved in their complete and original form, found in a timely fashion, that care was taken to preserve the records intact, and that they were managed after being found with controls to limit access to them for integrity purposes.

7) **False.** Remember Arthur Andersen? That firm is, for all practical purposes, out of business over this precise problem. Record keeping rules are essential and so is the need to have a separate Legal Hold policy. They are totally different. The former provides the rules for regular management of records in normal business times. The latter is to ensure that any and all potentially relevant information, documents, and records are preserved when litigation, audit, or investigation seems imminent or is commenced. In essence, the Legal Hold is the termination of regular retention and replacement with new rules that mandate preservation. Following the completion of a lawsuit, investigation, or audit, the Legal Hold is terminated. It is at this point that the regular Records Management policies and

retention rules once again apply. However records preserved may be subject to more than one Legal Hold, so before disposing of any records make sure that **all** Legal Holds affecting those records have been reviewed and terminated. Never rush to purge records following a Legal Hold termination, especially if it is reasonable to expect that the records may need to be available for a subsequent matter.

Ensure That Legal Responsibilities Are Clear— Especially When Trouble Strikes

> *"Although it did not do so willfully, maliciously, or in bad faith," the defendant allowed e-records required to be preserved in the context of the lawsuit to be "destroyed during routine deletions of computer information."*
>
> Applied Telematics v. Sprint[43]

A telephone company is sued. Electronic records are requested. However, when the company tries to locate them, the records are gone. Why? Was it the nefarious action of a rogue employee seeking to cover his tracks? Did someone look at the records and decide that they contained harmful material that had to go away?

No on both counts.

In fact, the records disappeared as part of a routine purge or recycling of the storage media at the company. Apparently, no one had advised IT about the need to suspend the recycling procedure due to the lawsuit. Apparently, IT didn't get the memo, if there even was a memo.

The reality today is that more and more of what we do in the digital world—including the way we create, use, manage, and dispose of information—has serious legal implications. Moreover, in a world where each employee has the ability to create (or destroy) the thousands of electronic records they possess on their desktop computers and other devices, the need to ensure that everyone clearly understands their legal obligations has never been greater.

There are two major reasons that organizations need to have ready access to their information; 1) to run their business, and 2) to satisfy the legal obligation of making information available (even if it's harmful to their legal position) when requested in a lawsuit, audit, or investigation. Apparently this latter obligation of preserving and producing information in court proceedings or to regulators has been lost, as so many companies and individuals have been alleged to have destroyed evidence over the last few years. Given this reality, more than ever the Warrior needs to carry the message throughout the organization about IMC legal responsibilities and requirements. The need for this guidance is especially acute when the organization faces contemplated, imminent, or pending audits, investigations, or litigation.

The Legal Hold Challenge

A party is obligated to retain evidence that it knows or reasonably should know may be relevant to pending or future litigation. . .Obviously service of a discovery demand places a party on notice to preserve the materials explicitly requested, but the duty to preserve arises whenever a party has been served with a complaint or anticipates litigation.

Mathias v. Jacobs[44]

When the automobile was introduced, there was very little infrastructure to support it. The "rules of the road" were not adequate to support the faster, heavier, noisier contraptions. But, slowly, as the automobile became an integral cog in the machinery of everyday life, that infrastructure did develop. Over the course of more than one hundred years, laws, regulations, and policies matured and evolved, and continue to evolve today.

In much the same way, the laws, regulations, and policies surrounding the use of electronic information in the legal context continue to evolve and grow in sophistication. According to one court, "[c]omputers have become so commonplace that most court battles now involve discovery of some type of computer-stored information."[45] With the burgeoning amount of electronic information in most every organization and the corresponding obligation to manage and perhaps produce it for a lawsuit, questions are now being asked and answered by courts daily. What does that mean for an institution with thousands of employees and thousands of computers spread across the country or the world, and millions of voice mail, email, and instant messages a day?

The simple fact is that when an organization is involved in, or anticipates that it will become involved in, a lawsuit, an audit, or an investigation, regular record keeping rules need to change. Any disposition or alteration of information potentially relevant to the proceeding must stop immediately.

The Legal Hold Process

Organizations should employ a process designed to notify employees of the need to preserve information related to a lawsuit, investigation, or audit. This process is commonly referred to as a "Legal Hold," "Document Hold," "Litigation Hold," or "Records Hold." The process should be described in a written policy.

Warriors should develop a Legal Hold process that includes:

- A policy specifically for the Legal department regarding their responsibility to provide a Legal Hold notice to the rest of the organizations' employees and the circumstances and timing of providing such notice.

- A separately written company policy outlining employee responsibilities and preservation procedures. What the lawyers are required to do in the context of a lawsuit, audit, or formal investigation will be different from what the rest of the employees will have to do. So don't confuse the employees by melding both policies in one.

- A standardized method for providing the Legal Hold notice to employees. Legal Hold notifications should be as clear as possible and stated in plain English so that all employees will understand what is required. Refrain from legalese to the extent possible.

- A statement from executive leadership in operations or training manuals that clearly expresses the company's commitment to records and information management compliance. In policy, training, and on a periodic basis through other mediums, it is prudent to remind employees of their further obligation to preserve any information that is even potentially relevant, even if it hurts the company. If employees are going to "listen" to anyone they are likely to listen to executives, so make sure the executives "speak" on this topic often.

- A training program to educate employees about their preservation and retention responsibilities, with updates on new legal and regulatory requirements, and their responsibilities relative to these changes.

- Audit or spot check procedures to make sure employees are following the policies. Recent court cases make clear that just sending out one notice to employees to preserve may not be sufficient. In addition to sending reminder notices, you need to check that employees are doing what they are supposed to.

The Legal Hold Notice: A Checklist

When writing and issuing the Legal Hold notice, the Warrior should address the items in this checklist:

- Send the Legal Hold notice to employees likely to have responsive materials. Unless the matter impacts the whole company don't send the notice to everyone. The "shot gun" approach to distribution can undermine the process by overwhelming employees with so many notices that when they need to take some action they fail to.

- Spell out what's required of employees in plain English. For example, "Do NOT destroy, revise, alter, hide (by encrypting or otherwise), or move company records."

- Be specific about which records need to be preserved— records, documents, and drafts (paper or electronic) created within a specific time period that are about a particular product, customer, or business deal. Clarify the need to preserve relevant documents normally scheduled for disposal according to standard retention guidelines.

- Do **not** include any privileged information or a lawyer's analysis about the merits of the matter as it could undermine the Attorney-Client Privilege.

- Provide the responsible lawyer's contact information in the notice so any questions can get addressed immediately.

- Contact affected business unit leadership as they will likely know who may have information that needs to be preserved or know how to get it.

- Communicate directly with key players responsible for discoverable information on a consistent basis—a blanket statement to all personnel may no longer be sufficient.

- Retain evidence of having sent a clear message describing legal obligations and employee responsibilities to show good faith efforts on the part of the organization.

- When the matter is concluded, send employees a Notice of Termination of the Legal Hold and indicate that regular record keeping rules once again apply. Remember that information may be subject to more than one Legal Hold so verify if other pending matters require the information to still be preserved. Above all else, never rush to destroy, no matter what.

Manage Information Today— Prepare for Tomorrow

Warriors must help their organizations prepare for the discovery process in advance. The organization must know what electronic information it has, where that information is located, and how it might best be corralled and managed.

- **Enable ready access to information.** Failing to produce records quickly enough can have serious repercussions and may be viewed as purposely failing to cooperate. A prominent securities firm recently faced a Securities and Exchange Commission (SEC) probe in which it provided only a "small fraction of the responsive emails" six months after the initial request, and did not produce all relevant documents until two years had passed. Investigators repeatedly objected to the rate at which the emails were being produced, informing the company that they were failing to meet the SEC's expectations. Ultimately, the SEC penalized the company $10 million, an amount that might have been considerably less if the organization had produced requested information more quickly.[46]

- **Bolster long-term access to legacy records.** Document where records can be found so they can be viewed and produced even several years down the road. Include in your documentation the technology requirements that must be met to ensure legacy records can be produced after new hardware and software versions are implemented. Ensuring access may require maintenance of obsolete hardware or software tools that have no use in active business operations but are needed to access or restore old records information.

What Kind of Information Should You Be Prepared to Produce?

A discovery dispute in a recent case illustrates the extent to which an organization's computer systems can be subject to a discovery request. The plaintiff in this case argued that the defendant had breached their software agreement, believing the defendant had illegally attempted to combine the plaintiff's proprietary software with other software tools. The defendant was ordered to preserve backups of all systems that contained any part of the software and related materials in question, and preserve backups of their email servers, pending further orders. This included, "any associated software, whether used for development, production, or otherwise, including source code, object code, history or log files, or revision tracking files."[47]

Make Informed
IMC Legal Decisions

As the telecommunications industry was deregulated over the past couple of decades, consumers gained the ability to choose their telephone company. There was a negative side to this new freedom, however, with some firms unscrupulously switching a consumer to their service without the consumer's full knowledge or consent.

To combat this practice, known as "slamming," the U.S. Federal Communications Commission (FCC) passed Anti-Slamming regulations, which among other things, require telecommunications carriers to seek a subscriber's clear permission to change or update their service.

In 2000, the FCC ruled that this process could be completed on the Internet, but added the caveat that,

> . . . *if a subscriber contests the authenticity of [the process], the carrier **will have the burden of proof to counter the subscriber's allegation.** For this reason, we would expect a carrier to employ procedures that would enable it to demonstrate that the electronic signature [used] could not have been submitted by anyone other than the subscriber. [emphasis added]* [48]

The requirements outlined in this regulation demonstrate a key point. The regulation makes clear that the digital process must authenticate the subscriber and that the company must be able to prove that authentication, but the regulation **does not tell companies how to build a process that will accomplish this.** It is up to the firm, therefore, to determine how to build and implement a process that complies with the regulation.

The same principle is carried through many laws and regulations that impact IMC. Key practical, procedural, and technical decisions are left up to you, the Warrior. The Warrior must understand the difference between what the law requires and what decisions are left to the organization.

Electronic Records and Signatures: Where the Rubber Meets the Road

> ... the essential attribute of a signature involves applying
> a sound, symbol or process with an intent to do a legally
> significant act. It is that intention that is understood in the
> law as a part of the word "sign," without the need for a
> definition.
>
> The Uniform Electronic Transactions Act[49]

Lawmakers around the world have acted over the past two decades to clarify the legal admissibility and acceptability of electronic records and signatures. U.S. federal and state laws now allow electronic records and signatures to be used in place of their paper-based counterparts for more purposes than ever before. Electronic records can be offered as evidence in most legal jurisdictions without fear that they will be rejected simply because they are not in paper form. Indeed, laws regarding evidence generally do not require records to be in any particular form. Furthermore, electronic records can be used to satisfy the recordkeeping requirements of an increasing number of federal and state regulators.

Two of the key U.S. laws in this regard are the federal Electronic Signatures in National and Global Commerce Act (E-SIGN),[50] passed in 2000, and the Uniform Electronic Transactions Act (UETA), which has been adopted by the majority of the states since 1999. Both of these laws work to put digital records on par with paper records and to clarify that electronic records and signatures cannot be discriminated against for regulatory and evidentiary purposes merely because they are in digital form.

However, these laws do not diminish requirements that electronic records and signatures are created and managed in a manner that promotes trustworthiness. Further, these laws rarely specify the methods, processes, or technologies that should be used to create electronic records and signatures in a way that will comply with the law.

For example, consider how UETA states its requirements for electronic records that are sufficient to meet legal obligations:

> (a) *If a law requires that a record be retained, the requirement is satisfied by retaining an electronic record of the information in the record which:*
>
> > (1) *accurately reflects the information set forth in the record after it was first generated in its final form as an electronic record or otherwise; and*
> >
> > (2) *remains accessible for later reference.*"[51]

Clearly, this definition is the furthest thing from a roadmap for building a system that creates good electronic records and requires the Warrior to make a host of decisions about electronic records management.

Consider the definition of electronic signature provided by E-SIGN:

> *The term "electronic signature" means an electronic sound, symbol, or process, attached to or logically associated with a contract or other record and executed or adopted by a person with the intent to sign the record.*

Again, this definition provides little in the way of practical, technical direction for Warriors building, purchasing, or evaluating compliant systems.

Making Decisions About Electronic Signatures

Can a mouse click on an online button really be binding?

Yes, but it has to properly planned, implemented, managed, and retained. To satisfy law as it relates to a "click wrap" signature (one created when a user "clicks" in a specific area of a software application to indicate intent), the Warrior will have to address the following:

- **Significance.** Give the users every opportunity to understand that by clicking on a button or graphic reading "I Agree" or something similar, they are doing something as significant as signing their name on a piece of paper.

- **Opt-out.** Inform users of their right to withdraw from the digital-only process, and of any right they have to receive paper copies of information in addition to the electronic information.

- **Replacement.** Clearly explain that by clicking "I Agree," the user is consenting to receive information related to the transaction in electronic form instead of in paper form.

- **Security.** Treat private information confidentially, regardless of whether it is in paper or electronic form. The process for assigning "electronic signatures" (such as an ID and password) to the users for accessing online accounts and other services must be secure.

- **Technology requirements.** Clearly explain what software and hardware users will require to access, print, or locally store their electronic records generated by the process. There may be requirements to provide users with the technology they need.

- **Forced path.** Prevent the users from circumventing or taking a "shortcut" through the series of screens, dialogs, and other devices used to impart the required information. Capture their actions as they navigate to prove that users have received the information that they require in order to provide informed consent to the process. The goal is to capture convincing proof of what the users saw, when they saw it, and what they agreed to.

This list of requirements should make clear that Warriors need to balance legal requirements, technological capabilities and limitations, user considerations, records management best practices, and business interests when making the practical decisions required for compliance. The Warrior is uniquely positioned to have the range of knowledge required to guide their organization through these decisions.

Click Wrap Signatures: In Practice

A construction company purchased and used proprietary software to calculate its bid for a government contract, only to discover that the software they used mis-stated their bid by $1.95 million.[52] When the construction company sued the software vendor for breach of warranty, citing defective software, the court found that the vendor's end user license agreement's limitation of remedies clause completely protected the vendor despite problems with the product—even if the purchaser never saw the clause or the software company was aware of problems with the product prior to sale.

Since by some estimates, more than 50% of business software purchases are non-negotiable shrink wrap (named for the plastic shrink wrap packing around most off-the-shelf software) and click-wrap transactions, it's critical that organizations make careful choices and consider the laws that affect purchasing when entering into agreements for goods or services intended to play a vital role in business.

Don't Try to Buy Compliance

Software companies have lost no time trying to market Sarbanes-Oxley products and tools. But CIOs should look before they leap into purchasing these supposedly ready-made answers. It isn't easy to put compliance in a box.

Eric Nee, CIO Insight[53]

The words "expensive software implementation" are not synonymous with compliance. The Warrior knows that IT can provide the tools to automate, support, and improve the compliance process—but cannot provide compliance itself. If your organization's IMC program has holes, technology solutions won't stop company records from falling right through them.

Warriors will keep the following tips in mind when addressing their organization's IMC challenges.

Avoid Legal Advice from a Salesperson

When it comes to IMC, the Warrior should seek legal advice only from qualified professionals. Hardware and software vendors are not generally qualified to provide legal advice. Do not rely upon them to answer your IMC legal questions and solve your IMC legal problems.

Rely on your vendor representatives for what they are good for—providing information about their products, on how they might help you, and on how they have helped others like you. Salespeople might also be a great resource by pointing you in the right direction for the legal and compliance resources and advice that you need.

The person "selling you" on a compliance solution may be someone who works in your IT department. Internal IT departments can be just as aggressive as vendors in promoting IT solutions, and their proposals should be similarly scrutinized.

Validate Compliance Claims

The Warrior should validate compliance claims made by vendors. Have your lawyer review the vendor's product literature and invite Warriors from legal and other departments to participate in vendor pitches. Discuss vendor claims around compliance with your information management committee and company experts. Contact customer references provided by the vendor and ask to speak with legal or compliance staff at those firms.

Keep in mind that there may be simpler and less expensive solutions to your compliance problem than IT implementation.

Carefully Evaluate "Intelligent" Solutions

Warriors should seek out solutions that are designed for their organization's unique IMC challenges. Automated retention software may be a true panacea for some organizations that must sort through massive volumes of data to process and maintain valuable company records. But as useful as these automated solutions may be, keep in mind that "artificial intelligence" tools, under the best case will likely fail a certain portion of the time.

If software tools are used to support IMC, they should be audited regularly to be sure important records aren't slipping through the cracks. Can the software vendor provide you with statistics that reflect the success rates of classification using their product? Is the product tailored to the needs of your organization, or might expensive add-ons or fixes be required to make it run effectively?

The idea of a hands-off, transparent approach to electronic records retention where employees don't have to make conscious decisions and compliance is "assured" is undoubtedly appealing—but what success rate is acceptable? Ninety-five percent? Ninety-nine? Could a court live with hearing that your company fails to retain e-records properly 25% of the time?

As you evaluate and choose technology solutions for IMC, make sure to consider potential legal pitfalls and get the vendor to verify performance claims. You don't want the courts to be the ones uncovering system failures.

Fight the Urge to Buy into the "SOX in a BOX" Solution

Sarbanes-Oxley compliance requires a new perspective that has more to do with adjusting business and accounting practices than any technology implementation. While there are legitimate reasons for "fear, uncertainty, and doubt" around SOX, be wary of software products with exaggerated claims of solving all of your SOX compliance.

Before considering an IT solution to address Sarbanes-Oxley IMC issues, the Warrior should ask the following:

- Does the organization devote the proper resources to managing information? Is there someone like a Chief Compliance Officer that has leverage to ensure requirements are met?

- Are processes in place to reliably audit and document information security measures to ensure the immutability of company records?

- Are financial reporting and disclosure methods accurately tracked and audited to back up executive certification of annual and quarterly reports and internal controls?

- Can existing software be tweaked to handle the organization's compliance needs, rather than investing in a new software package?

There are situations where new IT solutions may be the only way to address SOX compliance. Real time reporting to investors or tracking disclosure methods with audit trails for proper documentation, for example, may require investing in new technology.

However Sarbanes-Oxley impacts your organization, it is important to view technology as one tool in the SOX toolkit, but not to see it as the Swiss Army knife that can do it all. Organizations should pay just as much, if not more, attention to the non-technical means of relieving SOX headaches.

Answer true or false.

1. Regulatory and quasi-regulatory bodies will never tell your organization what technology to use or not use.

2. The California Database Protection Act affects only private companies located in California.

3. Sarbanes-Oxley impacts what information you make available on a website.

4. You cannot be held responsible for the malicious acts of hackers.

5. Regulators may get angry and may impose penalties but they will never impose an invasive corrective action when you fail to manage information properly.

Answers

1. **False.** While the law has evolved to be technologically neutral (the laws or regulators will not tell you what technology to use), recently a federal authority advised financial institutions against using instant messaging given the security threats. Other regulators have made and will likely continue to make similar technology guidelines in the right circumstances.

2. **False.** This state law impacts public and private organizations that have protected personal identifiable information of California residents, no matter where the organization is located.

3. **True.** According to SOX, for disclosure purposes, certain company stock transactions have to be posted to company websites within days of the transaction.[55]

4. **False.** Your organization can be held responsible for failure to properly secure IT systems, have updated protections, or lose control of information. A new California act imposes responsibility on "innocent" organizations when certain information is disclosed even through the criminal acts of a hacker.

5. **False.** When makers of a drug failed to follow their own privacy policy, the Federal Trade Commission imposed a very invasive and onerous privacy management regime on the company. It is probably a lot less painful and cheaper to be proactive with IMC and do it yourself.

Strive for IMC Consistency

18

Warriors should seek consistency throughout the IMC program, including the way that policies and procedures are written, the way that the program is enforced, the way retention rules are applied, and the way that employees are trained.

The law likes consistency. Even at the level of the individual record, the law prefers those created as part a routine, consistent business process. Consistency points to forethought, to planning, to careful action, and ultimately to reasonable conduct because the same rules apply across the board. Consistency helps to demonstrate that IMC is taken seriously throughout the entire organization.

Train Your Organization

A recent survey reported that only 35% of companies deliver regular employee training on records and information management issues.[56] These numbers reveal that IMC is often inadequately addressed where it matters most—with the ground troops that interact with company information on a daily basis.

Regular IMC training is key to addressing the ever changing regulatory and legal requirements. An organization's culture of responsibility in regard to IMC must be conspicuous to employees. More importantly, all employees must fully understand the role they play in meeting compliance standards.

Regular training might include the following themes:

- **Industry updates.** How are evolving IMC issues and practices affecting your organization and others in the industry? How is your organization going to address new challenges and requirements?

- **End user specifics.** What systems require special attention to retain company records? Do you retain e-records from portable devices? What is the employee's role if required to store documents at the local level?

- **Legal Hold.** What should employees do in the event of a Legal Hold? Are employees responsible for notifying the law department of potential developments that could lead to litigation or company audits?

Leave A Message After the Beep . . . Oh, Bleep!

Two companies were involved in contract negotiations. During the negotiations, a group of lawyers and officers from one company phoned the other on a speakerphone for a conference call. Nobody answered the phone, so, they left a message. They then continued to talk amongst themselves—without hanging up the speakerphone. Their entire conversation was recorded by the voicemail system at the other end.

Embarrassing, but no damage done, right?

Wrong.

What did the voicemail system capture the little group talking about? How they "did not intend to abide by the terms of the contract" and how they planned to steal "trade secrets and hire away [the other company's] key employees."[57]

Consistency Starts at the Top

Statements from executive leadership concerning IMC policy and practices won't replace policy or regular training on IMC issues, but they go a long way toward reinforcing a culture of responsibility and good faith on the part of the organization. Statements regarding the leadership's stance on records and information management should be standard in employee training or operations manuals and should include the following:

- That IMC is a priority to the organization, is taken seriously, and all employees no matter their business unit or level in the company play a role in maintaining compliance

- Potential penalties for failing to adhere to company policy

- Contact information for individuals who can answer employee questions concerning records and information management

Instant Messaging

Instant messaging (IM) is used in 85% of organizations across North America. By the end of 2004, there will be over 350 million business users of instant messaging, generating 11.4 billion messages each day (growing to over 45 billion in 2008).[58]

IM is a popular tool because it's quick, it's easy, it's almost as real time as a phone call, you can work while you wait for a response, you can instantly transfer files, and it saves on long distance charges. So what's the problem?

The problem is that IM isn't taken seriously as a business tool and it is one of the least managed electronic communications tools in organizations today. For example, a recent survey found that only 21% of organizations had a formal written policy regarding IM.[59] IM slid into the business world by accident. Employees already familiar with IM from personal use often installed it on their work machines without permission. Many company policymakers are unaware of the extent to which IM is used in their own company for business purposes.

Some organizations, however, are getting the message that unmanaged and unregulated instant messaging exposes computer networks to unnecessary risks. The Federal Deposit Insurance Corporation (FDIC) recently issued guidance to financial institutions on the effective use and management of instant messaging.[60] The letter warns banks against using workplace IM without considering the potential privacy and security risks. For institutions to benefit from IM without placing information assets in jeopardy, the FDIC suggests using an official corporate instant messaging client that can "authenticate, encrypt, audit, log and monitor" employee communications.

Thoughtful implementation of the appropriate instant messaging software should be part of a larger enterprise effort to address big-picture security concerns. The FDIC recommends that banks perform a risk assessment on the benefits of IM, develop an IM policy, and configure systems to defend against potential vulnerabilities in instant messaging software. On a separate but related note, the SEC and NASD also have rules for the brokerage community that require specified email and IM communication to be retained.

These recommendations are useful to all Warriors guiding their organizations on the use of IM:

- Develop IM policy and procedures that cover acceptable use as well as information security and retention issues.

- Restrict the use of instant messaging to a secure and closely monitored corporate software client.

- Configure systems to detect remote intrusions and block unprotected file sharing through IM software.

Instant Messaging (IM) Disclaimers

"By participating in this forum you consent to having your communication recorded"

An FBI agent posing as a minor entered into communications with a suspected child molester through an instant messaging tool, preserving the conversation by cutting and pasting text from the program into a word-processed document.

However, the evidence they gathered was found inadmissible because current wiretap laws in New Hampshire and other states require consent from all parties involved in a conversation for that conversation to be recorded.[61]

So how does the case apply to your organization? Consideration and application of the legal principal advanced by this case is prudent even if the facts of the case will never be applicable to your situation. If your organization is using IM to do business and may need to capture IM records, it might be advisable to notify users that by using IM, they are consenting to all IMs being recorded and reviewed by the company.

- Ensure security through effective virus protection and patch management tools.

- Address the risks of IM use in regular information security training for employees.

Dealing with the Tough-to-Retain Records

It is no small matter to retain various types of electronic communications in electronic form, or any form for that matter, and make them retrievable like any other company records. So what is a company to do? Consider the following approaches:

- Disallow the use of some technologies. A drug company recently undid its PDA program, costing millions, because the company lost control of its information.

- Tell employees to refrain from using the technology for any company business communications that would rise to the level of being a record.

Apply Rules Consistently to Paper and Electronic Records

In a recent case involving allegations of police misconduct in Columbus, Ohio, it was found that the city had properly disposed of paper copies of police disciplinary records in accordance with its retention schedule, but had not disposed of the electronic versions.

As a result, records dating back almost 10 years were still available and the court decided that they could be accessed by the public.[62] Following this decision, another lawsuit was commenced that pitted the Police Union against the City for failure to consistently apply the retention rules to the electronic records.

Rules must be applied consistently to all records, regardless of their format.

- For communications that do rise to the level of being a record, develop policies that require the recipient employee to transcribe the communications in paper form with all the necessary transmission information and retain like all other paper records.

- Find a way to retain the record electronically, but make sure it is done in a way to ensure the record has integrity.

Consistency Checklist

Warriors should take the following steps to ensure consistency in their IMC program:

- Evaluate the importance of all records according to their content and significance, regardless of format. Don't neglect to retain business records that live in "informal" environments, such as email, voicemail, instant messaging, Web blogs, or discussion groups. Many companies have started advertising in Web blogs. The laws don't say you need to retain records of your business except ones found in Web blogs. Just because they are casual environments does not mean records can't be found there.

- Review all information related policies and make sure your organization deals with content consistently no matter the form or medium of the content. Employee healthcare records, for example, need to be secured whether they are in paper or electronic form.

- Retain different record types consistently, regardless of location or the media on which the record is preserved. The haphazard disposition of records depending on how they are stored can put the organization at risk.

- Address the disposition of record originals, drafts, and all copies to prevent unnecessary storage of duplicate information—plus later retrieval costs.

- Dispose of data that's reached the end of its lifecycle in a systematic way, addressing all devices and storage media.

You May Not Like It, but You Still Need to Comply

The Warrior understands that legal and regulatory compliance is not voluntary. When the courts or regulators come knocking, failing to comply is not an option. When the law changes, adapting to the changes is not voluntary—no matter how unclear or onerous the change may seem. Unlike best practices, where organizations can comply as they choose, laws and regulations cannot be ignored.

The Warriors' role is to help their organization understand and appreciate the importance of legal and regulatory compliance across all of an organization's IMC activities.

What Do Legal and Regulatory Compliance Failures Look Like?

Case #1: Insurance Firm Fined and Forced to Create New Information Management Program

In a class action suit against a major insurance company, the court instituted a preservation order for both parties to retain all documents relevant to the litigation. When it was found that discoverable documents were destroyed at four of the insurance company's branch offices, the plaintiffs sought sanctions.

The court found that the destruction of evidence was not intentional or done in "bad faith," but rather blamed the company's preservation attempts and lack of a comprehensive retention program as "grossly negligent."[63] The court ruled that the failure resulted from senior management's failure to properly notify employees of preservation efforts and imposed a penalty of $1 million, as well as an extensive list of requirements to prevent further e-discovery failures.

The court required the company to:

- Mail a copy of the court order describing the new preservation requirements to every employee.

- Provide a revised policy and plans to distribute the new retention policy to all employees in the organization.

- Install a hotline to report document destruction to senior management.

- Reinforce preservation efforts by requiring the organization's field managers to certify preservation compliance.

- Reimburse plaintiff's fees associated with the plaintiff's filing for sanctions.[64]

In this case, the court went to great lengths to set the organization on the right track with regard to its preservation responsibilities. Organizations that fail to get their preservation efforts in line with what the law requires risk humiliating sanctions aimed at fixing the problem and sending the message that negligence won't be ignored.

Case #2. Accounting Firm Loses Most of its Customers Long Before it is Prosecuted

> *AARRGGH. Send more shredding bags. Just kidding.*
> *We ordered some.*
>
> Excerpt from Arthur Andersen
employee email message[65]

When Arthur Andersen was charged with obstruction of justice for shredding documents and deleting computer files, it instantly hurt the firm's bottom line. Clients started jumping ship before the case ever went to court and it wasn't long before the beleaguered firm began laying off workers and selling assets to rival firms.

Mired down by lawsuits, the company's damaged reputation sent its clients packing in droves and had companies carefully reviewing past financial statements to avoid a similar fate. Eventually the firm told the SEC they would stop auditing public companies.[66]

In the end, the criminal prosecution of the company sealed its fate.

Case #3: WorldCom Assigned RM Babysitter Because They Just Didn't Get It

> *"I'm not there to replace company management. I'm there to be the eyes and ears of the court."*
>
> Richard Breeden, former SEC Commission
Chairman, and WorldCom monitor[67]

A federal judge appointed a former SEC Chairman to oversee a fraud case against WorldCom, a major telecommunications company, for inflating its earnings by improperly booking $4 billion in expenses.[68] The SEC's official babysitter was assigned in part to keep the organization from destroying or mismanaging records related to the investigation.[69]

One Company's Failure May Be Felt Industry-Wide

Earlier this year, Federal agents conducted a search on the corporate headquarters and several campuses of a well-known technical school in multiple states. Officials at the headquarters stated they had no idea what the FBI was looking for, but that the government had requested a wide scope of information including student placement, retention, graduation, attendance, recruitment, grades, transfer credits, and records of graduate income. No allegations were made and no charges were brought against the company. Students were turned away and faculty questioned at ten campuses in different states.[70]

In response, stock of the parent company plunged 33%.

A few months later, the Department of Education revoked a school's ability to receive advance payments on loans in response to an SEC investigation into allegations that schools affiliated with the for-profit education company forged student records to collect loan money from the government. The company's stock fell 7% that afternoon.[71]

That same day, unrelated for-profit education organizations started to feel the heat resulting from SEC actions. Despite having no connection to the company under investigation, the stocks of three other companies fell about 4% that same afternoon.[72]

It's often the case that the actions of one organization can set off an avalanche of problems for the rest of their industry. In this case, the FBI's ears perked up in response to allegations. The net result of the ensuing investigations was damage to the entire industry through falling stocks and damaged reputations.

But we can learn from this trend. When you hear another organization in your industry is being investigated, make sure your policies, practices, and employee training have you covered, and learn from others' mistakes by closely following the events as they unfold.

> *. . . the preservation of [the data] would have required heroic efforts far beyond those consistent with [the company's] regular course of business. . . No business purpose ever dictated that they be retained, even briefly. Therefore, absent the violation of a preservation order, which is not alleged here, no sanctions are warranted.*
>
> Convolve, Inc. v. Compaq Computer Corp. [73]

Even with considerable effort to comply, it is possible to come up short. Smaller organizations may not always have the resources to cover all the bases, while large corporations may have the resources but face myriad complications in managing and retaining information due to their broad scope of operations, information, and personnel.

For this reason, the courts assess an organization's show of good faith when making determinations about an organization's actions. In the electronic discovery context, one way to establish good faith is to clearly communicate preservation responsibilities to employees throughout the discovery process.

In a gender discrimination suit against a prominent securities dealer, the defendant failed to produce discoverable emails requested by the plaintiff. In the protracted discovery dispute that followed, the court found that many of the emails in question had been destroyed, despite counsel having instructed the organization's employees to preserve relevant documents for litigation. The court concluded that the defense counsel should have taken steps beyond instituting a records hold and outlined these steps to ensure the organization would fulfill its preservation responsibilities in the future.[74]

1) The organization must institute a Records Hold when litigation begins or can be reasonably anticipated and must notify all employees of their responsibilities in this regard. Records Hold notifications should be reissued periodically to remind employees that certain records must be preserved.

2) Counsel should speak directly with key players involved in the litigation, as they will most likely have information relevant to the trial. These individuals should also be

periodically reminded of their responsibilities until the Records Hold is lifted.

3) Counsel must ensure the organization's employees produce copies of active files relevant to discovery and should sequester backup materials that house this information to separate them from records not pertinent to the case and keep them from being recycled.

The methods the court proposed to ensure good faith preservation efforts in this case constitute a commonsense approach to discovery. But individuals directly involved in litigation on behalf of the enterprise cannot assume that everyone in the organization has that common sense. Continue to communicate the relevance of preservation efforts to the organization throughout the litigation process to help employees understand what's required and to make preservation a priority.

The typical company must consult many state and federal laws when developing and maintaining their IMC program. Use of the Internet to conduct business has expanded the scope of applicable laws, by giving businesses access to customers all over the world. Where an organization **does business** is the issue now, not just where the organization is **located**. If your company services customers using the Internet, it may find itself subject to an increasing list of laws, regulations, and courts in other jurisdictions.

California Database Protection Act

Understanding an organization's information management responsibilities can be a complex process because what is required may vary under different circumstances. Federal law has provided some strong medicine to address corporate records management responsibilities in recent years, but state governments continue to interpret these responsibilities in different ways and some gaps still remain.

For example, there is currently no federal law in existence that requires organizations to contact individuals in the event of a security breach that threatens their personal information.[75] California, however, has stepped in to address the issue, leading the pack in protecting its residents from the dangers of identity theft in the electronic era with the California Database Protection Act.

This Act requires organizations to notify California residents of security breaches that exposed their protected personal information. The law recognizes the need to push beyond traditional geographical boundaries to protect customers of any organization that owns or manages unencrypted information related to California residents, even from organizations that do not physically reside in the state. The law warns that failing to notify individuals of unauthorized access to the protected information may result in liability, stating that, "[a]ny customer injured by a violation of this title may institute a civil action to recover damages."[76]

SOX and Foreign Companies

In a similar vein, but stretching legal requirements outside the nation's borders, the Sarbanes-Oxley Act (SOX) applies its stringent transparency rules to foreign companies that are publicly traded in the U.S.

SOX requirements of foreign companies (when traded on a U.S. stock exchange) include:

- That CEOs and CFOs of publicly traded foreign companies certify the accuracy of their organization's financial statements

- That these organizations develop internal controls to monitor accounting practices

- That foreign audit firms submit to U.S. investigations into their methods and practices when auditing listed foreign companies

The new requirements may have foreign businesses thinking twice before jumping into Wall Street, as compliance with SOX has greatly increased the cost of listing shares for trading in U.S. markets. Accounting experts estimate the average costs for the largest public U.S. companies at $4.6 million in the first year of SOX implementation, with average follow-on costs of $1.5 million annually.[77] Smaller businesses are hit even harder relative to their size, as the average costs of IMC for smaller public companies has risen 130% since SOX hit the scene.[78]

Test Your Warrior Quotient: One More Question

Failing to effectively manage your organization's information assets to meet its critical business and legal needs can cost your organization millions of dollars or damage its reputation from high-profile scandals or legal battles.

True or False?

If you didn't answer True, you haven't been paying attention.

---

warriorquadrant III

Business Quadrant

Carpe Diem: Making the Case for IMC Has Never Been Easier

The opening years of this new millennium have seen a series of business, legal, technological, and other developments that have dramatically changed the perception of records and information management. Whether through high profile business failures and frauds that led to new laws like Sarbanes-Oxley, or through the continuing expansion of our dependence upon IT for an ever-increasing volume of business transactions of ever-increasing value, the business community has started to wake up to the necessity of IMC.

The Warrior's role is to understand and leverage current events to help advance IMC within his/her organization. It has never been easier than it is today to make the case to business executives and management that IMC's time has come, and that IMC can and should play a central role in the organization's ongoing success.

The Changing Environment for IMC

Warriors need to become experts on how IMC relates to other activities within their organizations, but they also need to understand how broader developments in the business world impact the environment that IMC operates within.

The traditional challenge for IMC, from a business perspective, is that records and information management activities have been viewed as a necessary evil—a drain on the bottom line that adds little value to the organization. The perception has been that information management compliance cannot provide any leveraged value beyond its role as a tactical necessity.

Although recent events certainly haven't created a situation where business management is now "in love" with these activities, they have changed the perception of IMC's role within many organizations.

The reasons for this change are varied, and include:

- **Business has become more enlightened about the value of information.** Our cconomy is fundamentally information driven and business executives now understand that competitive advantage is inextricably linked to managing information more efficiently and securely.

- **Expectations have changed.** Today's organizations face a whole new set of expectations from the public, shareholders, regulators, courts, lawmakers, customers, partners, auditors, and boards about the way that information is managed. Today, good IMC is directly connected to good business management fundamentals.

- **IMC technology is maturing.** As organizations have begun to adapt to new expectations, the supplier community has responded with software and hardware products designed to support IMC management goals, from taking control of email to storing content in a secure and trustworthy manner.

- **Changing laws and regulations.** New laws, such as Sarbanes-Oxley and the California Database Protection Act, that stress the need for good IMC have been passed. Regulators have become newly aggressive in enforcing existing regulations that impact the way information is used, managed, and retained.

- **IMC is not seen as an isolated problem.** Increasingly, many organizations view records and information management activities as part of larger initiatives focused on compliance, good governance, corporate accountability, and transparency.

Start Thinking About IMC Like a Business Person

Although fear can be a powerful motivator for IMC, especially with many regulators and investigators pursuing aggressive enforcement agendas, Warriors also need to understand and articulate the value and business side of IMC. Consider the following issues and how they may be used to build your case for IMC.

- Are email systems bloated with unnecessary messages (e.g., duplicates, non-records) that bog down system performance? Are messages stored and indexed in a way that allows for quick and easy retrieval allowing the use of multiple search criteria?

- Does your organization deal with high volumes of employee records and job applications that could be managed more efficiently?

- Do employees, customers, and suppliers get the information they need as soon as they need it? Can IMC solutions also increase efficiency or customer satisfaction by providing relevant information faster?

- Are company records managed to ensure business continuity in the event of large-scale disruption of business practices?

- Is data building up in systems storage to the point that it frustrates the business process?

If Warriors use their unique perspective to sell IMC's ability to improve business processes, they will have a much easier time getting executive buy-in to IMC solutions.

This is not to say that today's Warrior will not still face resistance when working to convince executives to invest in an IMC program. From an economic perspective it is challenging to measure return on investment for IMC—even more so than for IT in general. Despite this, Warriors can learn to measure and report on the economic aspects of IMC, as explored in Chapter 9.

At the simplest level, the changing environment for IMC provides an opportunity for the Warrior to employ two basic strategies to promote and build support for the IMC program:

The Stick (Fear, Uncertainty and Doubt)

Well-known cases where information mismanagement played a starring role in a company's or individual's downfall (such as Andersen/Enron) have played a big part in changing the perception of IMC in the business world. For the first time, many executives came to understand that the result of information mismanagement could be drastic. Use well-known cases such as Andersen/Enron as a starting point, and build your own file of stories and cases that apply to your organization and its industry. (*Information Nation* provides details on a number of cases where organizations paid a steep price for IMC failures.)

A recent survey found that FUD (fear, uncertainty, and doubt) is the most popular technique used by IT professionals to convince their organization to invest in information security.[79] Warriors can use the fear that something bad might happen if the organization does not invest in IMC as a powerful motivator, especially considering the dramatic examples that are available. However, Warriors should be careful not to allow fear to drive bad decision making; good IMC decisions are made by balancing business and legal requirements—risk management not fear management.

The Carrot (Faster, Better, Cheaper)

> *"There is some ongoing benefit to using better systems, processes, and approaches for regulation to improve the performance of the business. That is the silver lining to regulation, which will be appreciated eventually. It seems a huge burden now, but sets the agenda for a better business. It is wrong to cast all regulatory change in a bad light."*
>
> Computing Magazine, October 2004[80]

IMC may have earned a new level of attention, but the likelihood of getting the program properly funded is much greater if the Warrior can align IMC with business strategies and operational improvements that save time and money. It's better yet if you can make the case that investing in information management compliance will bolster the bottom line.

The focus of IMC must extend beyond keeping the organization out of hot water. Warriors must set their sights on making a more efficient business by using their skills to leverage critical business information. Warriors must make the case for a more dynamic program, eschewing the image of the bespectacled paper pusher stowing carefully labeled documents in the dark corners of a warehouse.

A large financial institution made a commitment to digitize their customer files on a selective back-file conversion basis when files were requested. A simple plan with some simple technology. The result: questions and complaints by customers got answered during the first call, not three calls later. With information at the employees' finger tips, customers felt like they were doing business with a company that was helping them, not giving them the runaround. Employee time to address customer's queries decreased—as did the need for multiple calls and the need to ship original files around the country to research and provide a response. Happier customers are ones that do more business with your organization. The savings from the new process were calculable and real.

The more IMC can show up at the table with a valid business case, the more the organization will start to view it as a strategic asset instead of a cost center.

To help in this regard, the Warrior should:

- **Understand the business.** Warriors need to ensure that they have a solid grasp of their organization's business model, market, and strategic direction.

- **Stay current.** Stay on top of legal, business, and technological developments that impact IMC, and be prepared to help management understand the impact of these developments on the organization.

- **Gather supporting information.** Keep an eye out for news stories, case studies, whitepapers, and other relevant information that supports the case for IMC and helps to illuminate its value to the organization.

- **Share information upward.** Take the time to bring industry developments (and internal developments) to the attention of key management and project sponsors. Help them make their case upward as well.

- **Talk about victories.** When success happens and the economic benefits are felt, make sure that everyone, both up and down the chain, is aware of the success.

Use Business Management Techniques for IMC Success

The projects and activities that are part of building and maintaining an IMC program in many ways are no different than any project undertaken that requires the coordination of human, technological, financial, and physical resources. Warriors should learn to use standard business management tools and techniques to maximize the chance of IMC success.

Without good business management tools and techniques, IMC projects are just as likely—if not more likely—to blow through deadlines and budgets as any other project. IMC projects, because they rely on the participation and support from so many departments and areas of an organization, are particularly prone to these problems.

Warriors need to select and employ business management techniques that will help their IMC projects succeed, including those explored in this chapter.

Use Management Objectives to Stay Focused

Warriors should employ the simple, yet effective, technique of "management by objectives." Management objectives are simple statements of the top 3–5 priorities for an employee, workgroup, or department.

Management objectives should be specific, measurable, and time-limited. They should be regularly reviewed and updated to ensure that they reflect the organization's current goals and priorities, and support the overall plan for the IMC program.

Objectives not only help you stay focused, they are useful for decision making. When deciding how time and resources should be spent, the management objectives should be consulted. And unless an activity or task supports one of the objectives, little or no time or resources should be allocated to it, unless there is some very compelling reason. Management objectives can help overwhelmed employees stay focused and make good decisions about priorities.

Management objectives can also be used to measure individual employee performance. For example, the employee's performance against the objectives can be used to determine bonuses.

Warriors should use management objectives to align an IMC team's goals with the overall goals of the IMC program and to keep the team on course.

An example of a set of quarterly management objectives for an IMC team might include:

1) Update the retention schedule to incorporate the new Customer Relationship Management (CRM) system.

2) Deliver IMC training at European headquarters.

3) Release final Enterprise Document Management RFP with inclusion of specific IMC requirements.

4) Form an IMC Audit Council.

5) Prepare a presentation and report on IMC-related accomplishments for the Annual Meeting.

Clearly, this is an IMC team with a busy quarter ahead of them!

Regardless of the particular challenges that your team faces, spending the time to clearly outline your management objectives and obtaining upper management buy-in will go a long way to ensuring success.

Be Your Own Champion— Learn to Tell Your Story

Too often, good IMC work is overlooked by business management because Warriors have neither the skills nor the forum to communicate their success to the organization. Warriors need to learn to be their own "champions" by finding ways to convey their progress and success to management.

Warriors should take every opportunity to promote, discuss, and "sell" their work within the organization. This can be as simple as casual conversation at the water cooler or over dinner, or as elaborate as formal presentations and reports to large groups.

Warriors should use the following techniques to help IMC "get on the radar" of key executives and to build a positive perception for IMC across the organization:

- **Do your homework.** Research IMC solutions that address the needs of specific business units that fit with the organization's architecture and provide real value from a business perspective.

- **Be present.** Interact with leaders in the organization to learn what pressing business matters are getting the most attention. Make your presence known by linking IMC to these business issues.

- **Make your value known.** Sell IMC to your peers. Make them understand that IMC is a valuable tool for the organization and back up your claims with case studies and examples that illustrate how IMC can make business better.

- **Anticipate needs.** Learn about other areas of the organization and anticipate the IMC issues they are likely to face. Offer solutions to new problems before they've been fully addressed to make IMC a business problem solver and an agent of change.

One of our clients has developed a monthly electronic newsletter, which serves dual purposes. All employees get updated information about records management developments and it provides a regular report card about progress being made all the way to the corner office. In an indirect way, she tells management that she understands the importance and value of marketing the service and of continuous training on RM issues for the organization.

At a minimum, Warriors should strive to get on the agenda at key planning and management meetings. Even the briefest (but well-planned, rehearsed, and executed) presentation at such meetings can make a big difference in building awareness of, and support for, the IMC program.

Information that Warriors should highlight includes:

- Your management objectives for the month, quarter, and year and how well you did against them.

- Key projects and their status, especially those that have been successfully completed and where you can emphasize their timeliness and adherence to budget.

- External recognition of efforts provided by professional associations, trade groups, or media coverage.

- Internal "case studies" highlighting how your efforts or past projects—even those completed years ago—are paying off in the form of greater efficiency, improved process flow, lowered electronic discovery costs, etc.

- Keep your presentation brief and to the point.

- Use an appropriate tone and appearance for your presentation—model your presentation after those used by your senior executives.

- Be careful about using humor. That records management cartoon that everybody on the team loves might not be funny outside the workgroup.

- Think about what is important to your audience, not what is important to you. Your executives will likely not care about your classification system or detailed inventory plans, but they will care about how those initiatives provide a strategic benefit to the company.

Come to Management with Solutions, Not Problems

The Warrior needs to learn to think of the world from the perspective of solutions, not problems. In the IMC world, this can mean:

- Instead of asking for money to buy more disks to store email messages, request funds to develop a program that will educate employees on which messages they must retain and which they must dispose of.

- Instead of just forwarding a news story about an IMC disaster to your executive sponsor with the subject line, "Urgent! This could happen to us too," provide a brief analysis of the story's relevance, what you have done to address such risks, and a request for a meeting if there are immediate issues that need to be addressed.

The Warriors' job is to help their organizations understand and address IMC requirements and goals. Identifying **problems** is only half the job. Management will be looking to you to help craft the **solution** to the problem, so come prepared with potential alternatives.

Find an Executive Champion

Bob is a Records Manager for a Fortune 500 company, and he's as sharp as they come. He stays up nights dreaming of ways to improve the business and is constantly coming up with ideas on how to leverage the company's information to make business better.

But he's frustrated. He knows he has a responsibility to ensure good management of the organization's electronic records, but it seems he's always at odds with IT, who feel e-records are their responsibility simply because they're digital. The company's technologists think Bob should butt out and go back to the records room; so he does.

What's more, the occasional rumor trickles down to Bob's department, revealing failures in the organization's information architecture that cost the company time and money. He knows there's grumbling, both above and below, that information processing failures are hurting efficiency and customer satisfaction on multiple fronts.

Bob has some great ideas. So why doesn't anyone come to the records room and ask him for help? Surely they'll come one day—until then Bob can keep himself busy by filing stuff.

The problem with this scenario is that Bob has valuable expertise that can benefit his organization but hasn't thought of a way to "get it out there." There are people in the company who want to hear what Bob has to say, but he's got to sell records management to get their attention.

Bob needs an executive Champion—someone in the senior management structure that recognizes the value of records management, the expertise he can provide to other departments, and who has the ability to get Bob to the right people in the organization at the right time.

Warriors need to find Champions that share their vision for IMC, and can help to make it real. Partnering with champions has many benefits, including:

- **Source of resources.** Champions can obtain additional resources for IMC activities, not just in dollars but also in the form of human capital—new ideas, creative solutions, and greater leverage within the organization that can put a better face on IMC.

- **Business support.** A Champion can help flesh out a business case for IMC implementation that will best speak to executive leadership.

- **Implementation.** A Champion can help you gain inroads into specific business units or departments and use your success in one department to increase the prominence and implementation of IMC in other parts of the organization.

Finding the Right Champion

IMC projects are not always the most popular projects politically. Perhaps they remind executives of past mistakes or future problems they don't want to know about, are viewed as a resource drain and detriment to the bottom line, or perhaps they are the "pet" projects of an executive who is not well respected. This is all the more reason why IMC needs a champion at the executive level. In many cases IMC requires profound changes in the way that thousands of employees do their jobs—changes that simply will not be made without strong executive will and sponsorship.

While it is important to have a "titular" Champion—the person with the right title on his or her card—it is also important to have a "political" Champion. The level (or type) of power that an executive or manager holds in an organization may not be obvious from his/her title. Look beyond the title for people who have been around the organization for years and understand how things really work, for people who command respect because they are experts or really good at getting things done, for people who are not just receptive to change but have been change leaders. Among such people you will find your greatest ally, the perfect executive champion for IMC.

The Right Champion May Not Be Obvious

During interviews with several department heads at a Fortune 500 company, we discovered a Human Resources executive that had an interesting sideline—representing the company at regulatory hearings that had nothing to do with HR. When we asked why an HR executive was playing such a key role in the company's regulatory compliance, we discovered that he had been promoted from a compliance role into HR, but retained the part of his compliance job that he was good at and no one else wanted to do.

By looking only at the titles on business cards, we would have never understood who really was "holding the cards" when it came to compliance responsibilities. Similarly, Warriors should look beyond titles to understand "who really does what" inside their organizations.

Learn to Articulate the Business Value of IMC

The Warrior's job is to understand and articulate the business value of IMC throughout the organization. Even those who recognize the risk management value of IMC may be viewing its impact on a much smaller scale than what it's capable of.

Manage Information Overload

We are living in the "Information Age"—a period in history where information is central to all business processes. A common result is information overload. Despite a critical need to have the right information at our fingertips, individuals and organizations often find themselves swamped with data—some of it valuable, much of it useless. A well respected consulting firm evaluated how it was managing its information and concluded that "databases were teeming with outdated and unclassified information," which impacted its ability to run the business.[81]

This need for rapid access to valuable business information and the corresponding need to eliminate obsolete and unnecessary data can be used as one justification for information management compliance. The law does not require that organizations keep everything forever. IMC enables an organization to make "wheat and chaff" decisions about information—what stays and what goes—in a consistent and compliant manner. Getting rid of company information that no longer has business, operational, legal, compliance, or historical value as a "record" is especially beneficial in the electronic world. In today's organizations, where IT is critical to operations, processes, and strategy, clogging systems with useless information only steals from precious IT budgets and makes it more difficult to access the valuable information.

The Warrior needs to point out how those old boring retention rules have never been more important. Retention rules based on reasonable business needs and legal requirements allow the organization to keep what it needs and properly dispose of what it is no longer of value.

The **business** benefits of effective retention and disposition of records as part of an IMC program include:

- Preventing a drain on IT resources that can add costs and hurt performance
- Making needed records and information more easily retrievable by eliminating the need to search through high volumes of worthless information.
- Ensuring the disposal of records and information that have reached the end of their lifecycle to decrease ongoing management and retrieval costs.

Manage Information to Drive Business

Telemarketer: Good morning sir, this is Rob with your cable service provider . . . we are currently offering these 10 premium movie channels for only an additional $10 a month. Can we sign you up today?

Customer: We already subscribe to those channels.

Telemarketer: Oh, well . . . sorry to take up your time. Have a nice day.

Most organizations have powerful information assets at their disposal, but all the data in the world doesn't do any good if it's not effectively utilized. In the example above, the company has wasted a valuable opportunity to use information they already have in their possession—billing information—and have instead risked losing or at least alienating a good customer.

IMC can play a key role in helping organizations leverage their information assets by:

- Improving information access and customer response time with classification, indexing, and search tools
- Allowing for ready access to data through greater availability, proper classification, indexing and search tools
- Eliminating the use of outdated or incorrect information through effective retention and disposal policies
- Assisting with proper forecasting and planning
- Making information created for one purpose, such as billing, easily available for another purpose, such as sales and marketing

Manage Knowledge

In the Information Age, successful businesses are those that understand that knowledge is power—but only if the knowledge is leveraged. Knowledge cannot be leveraged unless employees have access to a broad scope of information to keep them informed, help to germinate new ideas and concepts, and improve collaborative relationships throughout the enterprise.

In many cases the organization's perspective on information sharing will come from the top. If executive leadership views information sharing as something that distracts frontline employees from fulfilling their duties, it could be a hard sell.

Since executive buy-in is critical, Warriors must provide a clear vision of how information sharing can help the organization. Too many organizations are still operating with the old "need to know" rule for sharing. In today's information-rich and constantly changing environment, the Warrior can make a good case for a "need to know why not" sharing rule.

Consider the value of a widely used calendaring function. For many information workers, meetings have become a significant portion of the workday. **Scheduling** those meetings can take a real toll on productivity in the time it takes to get everyone together. For companies that put their calendars online, the meeting can be scheduled in minutes, without even contacting the participants, because one person can find available time slots for everyone involved at the touch of a button. Online calendaring is a prime example of how relevant and updated information combined with open sharing policies can improve collaboration.

Allowing departments and business units throughout the organization to have an open view of each other's operations can have real value in creating opportunities for collaboration and more effective problem solving. Not only can information sharing bring new perspectives to bear on business issues and better arm business people to make informed decisions, but it can also improve interoffice relations and communications.

The benefits of enterprise-wide information sharing include:

- Integrating a decentralized organization
- Bringing an enterprise level perspective to day-to-day and critical decision making processes
- Improving awareness of the organization's goals and priorities
- Facilitating employee training and awareness of available resources.
- Allowing employees to better learn from the successes and failures of other parts of the organization
- Increasing the likelihood of innovation and refinement of existing processes
- And perhaps most importantly, making the place a more productive institution—doing business "faster better and cheaper"

Manage Change

24

Your organization is implementing a new IMC program. The program calls for considerable changes to the company's information management policies, IT systems, and the way that frontline employees handle information and interact with customers.

Consider this scenario: A new Customer Relationship Management (CRM) system has been approved for implementation and expected to cut costs and increase efficiency. Employees will be provided with customer information in real time—an improvement that should result in increased customer satisfaction with a corresponding increase in revenue. The system is also designed to ensure that customer information is collected and stored in a way that protects confidentiality and complies with privacy requirements.

Your company begins to promote the project by sending emails to employees, asking them to support the project and describing its benefits. Soon after the initial emails are sent, rumors begin to spread. Managers in some departments take issue with the project, believing it will make their jobs harder, and some employees believe the new system may put their jobs in jeopardy.

The fallout of this negative buzz impacts almost immediately. Representatives from all departments have been chosen for the project implementation team, but a few managers refuse to let their representative participate, claiming their departments are too busy. Some groups are slow to produce the documents and information needed to populate the database.

Finally, the organization holds an interactive webcast to discuss how the project will affect the company. The project team is overwhelmed by the negative response from employees and is largely unprepared to address employee concerns. Previous survey questionnaires indicated a relatively positive response to the project in its germinating stages, but now it seems the project has lost most of its support from internal customers. Hearing rumors of discontent, the CEO now wants to know what the problem is.

This project is in serious risk of failing.

What can Warriors do to prevent situations like this when they undertake IMC projects in their organizations?

Educate Executives and Middle Management

Top-down implementation is critical for any project requiring organizational change. Executive leadership sets priorities for the organization and must inform middle management and frontline employees that new initiatives are in fact priorities for the company.

A hands-off approach from executives won't do. Their stewardship of the project is essential in winning the support of middle management, whose potential negative reaction to the initiative may have the greatest effect once it trickles down to employees throughout the organization. That does not mean that executives will need to have day-to-day involvement. Rather they will need to lead the charge. Once momentum is moving in the right direction they can step back and allow others to carry the ball.

Your IMC team must communicate directly to middle management throughout the organization on a continuing basis, making sure all their questions are answered so they can reinforce new processes and directives to their subordinates. Middle management buy-in is essential to successful projects—their knowledge is critical to the specifics of departmental implementation and their authority over employees can either empower or hamper departmental buy-in.

Eliminate Resistance Through Widespread Involvement

Executive buy-in and middle management support for your IMC project is not enough by itself. Simply mandating changes from the top will result in mixed results at best. Policies, guidelines, and diagrams don't affect change; people do.

The organization's employees are the true "agents of change," and the Warrior must utilize them as such. Widespread involvement is key to making change as smooth as possible because it helps alleviate the number one obstacle to real organizational change—employee resistance.

Overcome employee resistance through careful planning and implementation of the following:

- **Be specific.** Don't just tell frontline employees that the change will benefit the organization. Clearly demonstrate how the change will make working for the organization better, easier, or more efficient for them.

- **Encourage ownership.** Involve all pertinent departments in implementing the change—inspire employees to take ownership of the process.

- **Anticipate problems.** Be prepared to address potential hurdles and try to work with would-be adversaries to address priorities that may differ from your own. Large scale organizational change may require a change in the organization's culture to engender new values in personnel.

- **Send the right message, and send it early.** The organization's policies and procedures must send a message to personnel that they too are "agents of change" and that the program is designed to benefit everyone in the organization.

- **Delegate effectively.** Delegate decisions to employees as much as possible to get them involved in and supportive of the process.

No matter the scope of the change, consistent two-way communication is essential in managing the people side of the project. Communications should be frequent—ideally a well-documented free flow of information that allows for knowledge sharing between all departments and levels of the organization.

Be patient? Are you serious?

"Be patient" is not something business people like to hear. However, large scale change takes time and may not happen in neat quarterly time frames. Managing real change is never easy; the more far-reaching the transformation, the more difficult it will be to implement. Whatever the obstacles, take solace in the fact that you're taking the organization in new directions and that your initiative will have an impact that will improve the enterprise in the long-term.

Align IMC with Business Goals

Every department within an organization needs to align their activities with the organization's high-level business goals and priorities. This is especially true with departments that serve the needs of a wide variety of internal customers; it is easy to lose focus when demands are diverse. Only through continuous realignment with organizational goals and priorities can such departments successfully fulfill their mandate over the long term.

Warriors must never forget this and must also maintain a realistic perspective. IMC is never going to be the most important thing that the organization does—nor should it be. IMC is an activity designed to support and promote an organization's business interests and to protect its legal interests. It is ancillary to what an organization does (unless the organization is a library).

In this respect, **IMC needs to undertake an examination of its relationship to business—much like IT has done in recent years.**

- Moving from a re-active to pro-active business role
- Keeping top projects on course
- Ensuring IT plans support business needs and strategies
- Evaluating how total IT performance affects business performance[82]

Warriors who diligently work to align their IMC activities with the organization's overall business goals can go a long way to ensuring that the program will receive the funding and support it requires to be successful.

Companies are not in business to win information management or compliance awards. They are in business to make money and they make money by serving their external customers. Businesses use a variety of methods to identify and communicate their overall goals and priorities. In the view of "Six Sigma," a management framework popularized in recent years, an organization's highest goal is to service its customers—and its success and failure are best measured against this goal. Some organizations use mission and vision statements to outline their overall reason for being. Setting priorities guides the organization and helps define the specific responsibilities of different business units and employees who must follow through on the organization's chosen goals.

Seeing Your World Through Their Eyes

In a recent survey, CIOs were asked to identify what they thought other executives at their company would view as top IT priorities. Their responses:[83]

• Lowering overall operating costs

• Acquiring and retaining customers

• Improving product and process quality

• Improving workforce productivity

• Managing business risks

• Driving new offerings or business practices

Warriors should consider conducting similar internal surveys to gauge the perception of IMC and the work of Information Nation Warriors, not only from executives, but also middle management and end users throughout the organization. Such surveys can reveal whether or not Warriors are doing a good job of "selling" IMC and of aligning it with business goals.

A powerful way to get your agenda across is to align it with the organization's high-level goals to the greatest degree possible. Warriors can do this by plugging IMC into what the organization cares about. If IMC isn't a clear fit with the department or business unit's current priorities, take it up a level and apply the discipline to the company's mission or vision statement.

Good Governance and IMC

Many organizations responding to the realities of today's business, legal, and regulatory climate have made investments in programs designed to support governance, responsibility, accountability, transparency, and business ethics. In some cases, enthusiasm for these kinds of programs is voluntary; in other cases, many elements of the programs are mandated by laws like Sarbanes-Oxley. In either case, governance programs typically have very high-level visibility and support within an organization, and Warriors would do well to understand how their work supports and advances such programs.

IMC plays a critical role in ensuring that organizations operate in an accountable way, and that they maintain the documentation and records that support accountable and transparent decision making. An organization needs to have confidence in the accuracy, reliability, and trustworthiness of its own records in order to make decisions and operate its business. IMC provides this confidence.

For example, IMC helps to ensure:

- Disclosures and representations made to boards, shareholders, regulators, courts, customers, and auditors are based on accurate and reliable information

- Senior executives have accurate and reliable information upon which to base key business decisions

- Intellectual property is properly managed and protected as a company asset

- Privacy of employees and customers is protected
- The organization can comply with laws and regulations (such as Sarbanes-Oxley and SEC regulations) regarding the management and control of information and the systems that house and create that information

Corporate Governance in the Spotlight

The U.S. Justice Department found that a major defense contractor mistakenly charged the U.S. Air Force $106 million for work on a commercial airliner and the testing equipment used in its development.

Subpoenaed records for the case revealed corporate management was involved in the decision making process that led to billing the commercial work to government-shared overhead accounts. Adding fuel to the fire, the company may have tried to sell the testing equipment it developed on the government's dime to third party airlines.

The company may face fines, penalties, and even criminal charges.[84]

Information is an Asset

Another key way for Warriors to align their activities with business goals and priorities is to adopt and promote the view that information is an organizational asset that must be managed and controlled like any other asset.

Adopting this view of information not only helps to demonstrate the value of information and IMC, but also Warriors' ability to view their work through the business lens.

Run IMC Like a Business

26

To a large degree, the work of the Warrior is going to be judged using business criteria, i.e., what did we get for our money? Warriors should anticipate these types of questions and judgments by independently applying such criteria to their IMC activities. In other words, the Warrior should learn to think of—and indeed, manage—IMC like a business.

Know Your Customers

Successful companies focus on the needs of their customers to generate sales and keep them coming back for more regardless of what the business is selling. Warriors also have a service to sell—IMC—and successfully selling IMC to the organization's internal customers is what differentiates a strategic IMC business solution from a tactical necessity.

The organization's departments (and business units) are the Warrior's customer base and they should be treated as such.

Most companies claim to provide excellent customer service—but unfortunately this often isn't the case. Many businesses don't fully understand what constitutes great customer service, which requires much more than a polite voice on the phone.

IMC Warriors are competing for limited internal resources and must know how to stand out in the organization. The good news is that by providing excellent customer service it's easy to stand out, because excellent customer service is really quite rare. Keys to customer service include:

- Building solid relationships with each department/business unit to enable more effective collaboration and reliance on each other's expertise.

- Delivering to each department/business unit what they want, not just what you think they need. If the internal customer's requests differ from what you think they really need, listen carefully and work to come up with a solution that satisfies all parties.

- Guiding department managers to the right solutions by showing them possibilities they may be unaware of. Offer a full range of solutions when possible and narrow down the choices to the ones that best serve the department's business needs.

- Maintaining open lines of communication with internal customers and making yourself available. If departments/business units can't get the help or answers they need, the organization runs the risk of "homebrewed" solutions, such as shadow IT popping up to solve workers' problems.

- Maximizing existing processes to provide internal customers with the resources they need. Processes that are effective and efficient are critical to good customer service.

- Taking employees' concerns, questions, and requests seriously and making an effort to gauge the success of worker satisfaction with IMC solutions on a regular basis.

Three years following the 9/11 attacks, more than 120,000 hours of terror-ism-related recordings from wiretaps and other intelligence sources had yet to be translated by FBI linguists, while newly recorded materials kept flowing in. What's more, the Justice Department reported that some Al Qaeda record-ings might have been accidentally erased due to computer problems at the Bureau. The investigation cited "antiquated and unwieldy" computer sys-tems as one root of the problem; limited file storage resulted in older audio files being deleted automatically to make room for new material, even if the older files hadn't been translated yet. In some cases, the bureau has had to go back and attempt to restore deleted recordings, and some file deletions might have gone unnoticed altogether.

The organization in this case has spent millions (perhaps billions) of dollars on what for them is a mainline "business" system—the interception and analysis of terrorist conversations. And yet, there is a fundamental breakdown in alignment between this "business" function and the groups that support the business function—in this case IT. The lack of communication, resulting in the deletion of un-translated information, completely frustrates the reason the application exists in the first place.

This lack of alignment occurs in businesses every day. The Warrior needs to work to ensure that IMC and business goals and activities are closely aligned.

Understand and Balance Business Needs

IMC is an activity that cuts across an entire organization and affects every individual, department, and business unit. To be successful, IMC programs must balance a multitude of compet-ing business interests and requirements.

The Warrior must remember that IMC may be viewed in a neg-ative light by many departments, particularly where executive support and an organizational mandate are not clear. Some IMC activities (such as email management) may require a substantial time commitment from employees and by extension, their departments.

In much the same way that most organizations are not in the business of IMC, neither are most departments. IMC is ancillary to the role that the department plays in the organization, and to the performance standards by which it is measured.

When architecting and implementing the IMC program, Warriors must learn to understand and be sensitive to the needs of these departments and the realities they face.

Building and Managing the IMC Team: Tips for Success

Many activities in IMC require collaboration with other Warriors throughout the enterprise. For example, the drafting and updating of an Enterprise Information Management Policy typically will require the involvement and coordination of attorneys, IT professionals, HR executives, business managers, compliance specialists, and senior executives.

The success of IMC projects depends in large part on the Warrior's ability to build and manage a team with the right skills, knowledge, mandate, and commitment.

Use the following tips to help your IMC work succeed.

Establish Both Strategic and Tactical Goals

It is important for the IMC team to establish both strategic and tactical goals. What is the difference between the two? Generally, strategic goals focus on longer-term, high-level achievements that depend upon the completion of several related goals. Tactical goals generally focus on specific, concrete activities that are more immediately addressed by specific actions.

For example, a strategic goal of "making the information management program more cost effective" might depend on the achievement of the tactical goals of: 1) hire Records Coordinators for each business unit; 2) consolidate east and west coast records centers; and 3) eliminate duplicate, legacy records management software.

Strategic goals are important for providing the IMC team with direction. Tactical goals tell the team how they are going to get there. Strategic goals should be developed in alignment with the business's overall strategic goals. Tactical goals should take into consideration current operating conditions and practicalities. For example, if the entire IT organization is focused on implementing a new Enterprise Resource Planning system for the next year, it is unlikely that a tactical goal of "implementing a records management software solution next quarter" will be achieved.

Pick the Low Hanging Fruit First

The Warrior should work with the IMC team to identify and address the low-hanging fruit—those issues that can be addressed the most expeditiously. Taking down the smaller problems first can help to build a track record of successes and grow "political capital" for when it comes time to tackle the big problems.

Low-hanging fruit are typically issues that meet **all** of the following criteria:

- Are causing consistent pain throughout the organization
- Have been recognized as a problem by several decision makers
- Have the least number of dependencies or "moveable parts" for support and approval

    (If the initiative is unlikely to get quick approval, it is probably not low-hanging fruit. For example, undertaking a redraft of the company's entire Records Management Manual, which requires the approval of 12 different executives, may not fit the definition.)

- Can be solved with existing technology and resources
- Already have the attention and support of senior management, or for which such support can be easily garnered
- Have easily identifiable viable solutions

Establish an Easy Way to Communicate and Coordinate

Having an easy way for every member of your IMC team to communicate, comment on drafts, and provide input will make your life much easier. Investigate existing collaboration tools that you may already have access to, such as networked areas for sharing files, group calendaring, or document revision and comment mark-up. These can be a great way to coordinate and get busy people in different locations to provide their input. Even a simple internal workgroup discussion list, where an email message sent to a group address is received by everyone who is part of the group, can be a simple way to make a big difference.

Establish a Clear Approval and Decision-making Chain

A project with no clear way to have its output approved and implemented amounts to little more than a good intention. Too much good IMC work goes to waste because no clear process for getting approvals and making key decisions has been put in place.

Find a Great Project Manager

The project leader is the critical success factor of a team. Not only is the leader responsible for managing the detailed tasks, she/he also has to be an excellent communicator within and outside of the team. Don't underestimate the importance of identifying the right person with both the technical background and mastery of the organization's culture to make the project succeed. Encourage your project leader to get a spot at high-level department meetings to provide progress updates that connect the project to the same set of goals that management is promoting.

How Important Is it to Have the Right People Engaged?

Two real life examples make the point.

1. A senior lawyer of a large public company has been not only intimately involved in the Records Management program development for years, but in many ways is seen as its champion. The problem is that she has started to be viewed as a liability because her colleagues view her as "chicken little." The lawyer's hysterical doomsday-ish view has become a liability for the program because others tune out her comments.

2. A financial services company has embarked upon a series of information management updates. The subject matter "expert" and project lead has been placed in the position because there is no other place for him. Additionally he is perceived as a "talker" and not a "doer" and not respected by the project team, which is made up of more senior staff. Having a project manager with this baggage is a major impediment to any chance of project success.

warriorquadrant IV

Records Management Quadrant

Make Value Judgments About Information

The destruction of evidence in the Government's pos-session, in this case an audiotape—particularly during times of national crisis—has the effect of fostering an appearance that information is being withheld from the public.

FAA Inspector General Kenneth M. Mead[86]

Six air traffic controllers that dealt with hijacked aircraft on 9/11 made tape recordings describing the events, only to see them destroyed without ever having been heard. The supervisor who destroyed the tapes said they were contrary to Federal Aviation Administration policy, which requires written statements and that the controllers were under too much stress on the day of the event to properly consent to the taping of official statements.

The tapes were destroyed despite an email message from the FAA asking supervisors to retain all materials related to the attacks. The email instructing New York managers to retain the records was unequivocal—"If a question arises whether or not you should retain the data, RETAIN IT."[87] The supervisor that destroyed the tapes was disciplined but potentially important evidence was lost. Even if destroying the taped evidence was not intended to hinder the investigation, the impression of a cover-up remains.

Warriors must guide their organization in making good value judgments about information. From an IMC perspective, organizations must assess the **value** of information based upon its **content,** regardless of its form, the media it is stored on, or where it is located.

A corporation cannot blindly destroy documents and expect to be shielded by a seemingly innocuous document retention policy.

Lewy v. Remington Arms Co.[88]

In a product liability case against a rifle manufacturer, the defendant appealed a previous court decision that sanctioned them for destruction of evidence. The defendant argued that the records in question were destroyed in compliance with its formal records retention strategy, and as such, the sanction was unjustified.

The three-part test applied by the court in this case can serve as a benchmark for Warriors to assess their own retention efforts and how they might be viewed in the context of litigation.[89]

1) **Is the organization's retention policy reasonable relative to the documents in question and the circumstances surrounding them?** What types of documents were disposed of and were they properly stored for a reasonable amount of time that reflects their significance and potential discoverability? As stated by the court, "A three year retention policy may be sufficient for documents such as appointment books or telephone messages, but inadequate for documents such as customer complaints," which may be required for litigation in the future.

2) **Have the documents or others like them been required for legal proceedings or investigations in the past?** Have similar lawsuits been filed in the past? If so, how frequently? Were the claims similar to the ones being advanced in the current case? If so, the same types of documents, records, and information that were used in the previous lawsuit may need to be retained longer.

3) **Was the document retention policy instituted in "bad faith"?** Did the organization suspect the documents might someday be used in a litigation and destroy them purposefully, "to limit damaging evidence to potential plaintiffs"?

On this last point, a court recently invalidated a records retention policy by concluding that the motivation for the new
policy was to try to legitimize the destruction of relevant evidence that was needed in a lawsuit. The court also focused
their attention on the fact that the policy was developed and
implemented contemporaneously with the lawsuit. So NEVER
develop a records retention policy or program to allow employees to clean house to make information unavailable for contemplated, imminent, or pending lawsuits, investigation, or audits.
Records retention programs should be developed to allow for
the efficient and expeditious retrieval of company records, not
as a means to obstruct justice, destroy evidence, or minimize
litigation exposure or costs.

A commonsense approach to recordkeeping will go a long way
in serving the organization's business needs, but a more refined
approach is often required to address how laws, regulations, and
the courts view an organization's retention responsibilities.

Assess the Value Based on Content

Organizations filter through high volumes of unimportant, unnecessary, and non-record data on a regular basis. There's no requirement
that says you have to "keep everything." Retaining documents and
communications that no longer hold business or legal value or are
not otherwise required to be retained is a waste of resources that can
make valuable information more difficult to find and put a drain on
system performance. The Warrior should set up retention guidelines
across the organization such as the following:

- Dispose of non-records once they've served their purpose.
  For instance, emails used to organize lunch dates or meetings should be deleted after the intended recipient has read
  the message or after the event has occurred.

- Duplicates and drafts of documents should not be retained
  unless there's a specific reason to do so.

- Optimize the retention strategy to filter out unnecessary
  non-record information before backing it up for business
  continuity purposes or long-term storage.

- Remember that even non-records are subject to discovery requests once litigation is anticipated. Do not delete seemingly useless documents or communications that may be even potentially relevant to a pending or imminent lawsuit or investigation.

Spam, Spam, and More Spam

Some experts believe that the increasing use of Internet telephony, commonly called Voice Over IP (VoIP), may provide spammers with a new means of disseminating unsolicited mail. Software now exists that can send voice messages to 1000 different numbers a minute. This potential Internet telemarketing explosion may pose new challenges for organizations. New software solutions may be necessary to avoid bloated systems and to facilitate efforts to separate company voicemail records from spam.

Mobile phones also pose new opportunities for spammers. A new Trojan Horse (a piece of malicious software code) was recently deployed by spammers in Russia that takes over PCs and uses them to send spam to mobile phones in the form of Short Message Service (SMS) text messages.[90]

Spam only adds to the challenge of filtering through the massive volumes of messages received by organizations today. The Warrior must plan to invest in the tools, technologies, and techniques that will limit the impact of spam on the organization—both today and tomorrow.

The Devil is in the Details: Metadata

Business has been quick to adopt information technology, but has been slow to apply Records Management concepts to the digital world. A business "record" created today is more likely to exist in an email message, a database, or a digital document than in paper form. Consequently, Warriors need to adapt their thinking about business records. It is the value of information in the record that matters, not the way the record is created or stored—a reality that must be reflected in the way information is managed across the organization. Failing to manage information according to its value has had—and will continue to have—profound business and legal consequences.

Imagine you are using a typewriter to write an employee evaluation. You go through several drafts trying to accurately assess the individual's performance, jotting down notes on a piece of scratch paper to help you sort out all the details. When finished, you hand the evaluation to your employee, proud of your work that accurately reflects her effort and attitude. But your employee becomes angry—all the notes you scribbled on scratch paper, much of it not so flattering, have somehow found their way onto the margins of the document!

Sound ridiculous? In 1998 a copy of the Starr Report that detailed an investigation of former President Clinton was made available to the public on the Internet. When the word-processed report was converted to HTML format for posting on the Web, it revealed footnotes that had been deleted from the document and were absent from the printed version provided to the U.S. Congress. The footnotes contained some embarrassing off-color comments, and soon made their way from the Internet to various newspapers across the nation.[91]

In another example, the British government published its findings on Iraq's security and intelligence organizations on the Internet in a word-processed format. Following the posting of the documents, a university professor discovered that portions of the dossier had been plagiarized. Sections of the document were taken almost verbatim from an article written by a post graduate student in the U.S., in one instance repeating a typographical error contained in the student's article.[92]

When managing records, the organization should make certain that metadata, the data about the data, is managed properly along with the message content and structure. Metadata may be an essential part of the record—for example the header of an email message. In certain circumstances, however, metadata may not need to be made part of the record. A client recently started using software to turn off the automatic logging of certain metadata. The client did not want the metadata to be part of the record since that would allow individuals outside the company to learn more about the creation of the record than was apparent on the face of the document. In any event, the decision to retain metadata as part of the record should not be left to chance.

Address the New Records Management Reality

The technological challenge is compounded by the continuing extension of information technology in terms of the type of information objects it produces . . . The resultant records are increasingly diverse and complex.

Kenneth Thibodeau, U.S. National
Archives and Records Administration[93]

Records today come in all shapes and sizes— in formats that even the most sophisticated IT professional may have difficultly identifying or understanding. These new kinds of records offer unique IMC challenges that Warriors must help their organization understand and address. New technology options will continue to spawn new complications. Simply stated, every time a computer is made part of a business process, there will be output that will require management. The worlds of Records Management and IT must intersect at a place that can adequately address these challenges.

Coordination with IT

Only by working together can Warriors meet the business, regulatory, legal, and operational needs of the organization. The IT department can benefit from understanding the perspective of the records manager, while the records manager must rely on IT's expertise to ensure the right records are retained in the right way. The following example—configuration of server access logs—illustrates how cooperation between Records Management and IT can benefit the organization.

The majority of computer servers, regardless of their operating system, have the built-in ability to monitor and generate records of users who have accessed applications and data residing on the server. These "log files" or "access logs" are typically configured and managed by server administrators for troubleshooting and security purposes. Most server operating systems also provide the ability to turn these access logs on or off and to configure the content of such logs in very detailed ways. Using these features must be limited to a certain degree, as logging excessive data can put a drain on system resources and provide more information than an organization is capable of storing and managing. IT generally turns on access log functions that are of use to them, turning off other log functions to conserve resources.

Beyond their typical use by server administrators, these access logs can play a vital role as they can establish a clear "audit trail," that shows when and by whom business records were created, printed, accessed, or changed. These access files, however, are not typically managed as records.

The RM Warrior should talk with IT about the specific use of log files to create audit trails of important records for legal and Records Management purposes.

The Importance of Intent

It can be difficult to define what constitutes a record in the electronic world. With digital information, it is possible to make an infinite number of perfect copies at little or no cost. So what differentiates an unnecessary copy from a record that needs to be retained? Should multiple copies be kept or does one suffice? Which copies should be kept and who should keep them?

One way to address these questions is by incorporating the concept of "intent" into the way that your organization defines company records. In a world where multiple copies exist, the "record" is the copy your organization intends to retain as the "official" copy.

For example, you send a contract as an email attachment to twenty people for review. Just sending the contract to twenty people as an attachment leaves you with potentially twenty-two "official" copies of the record—twenty copies in the respective inboxes of message recipients, one copy in the "sent items" folder of the sender, and the "original" document on the hard drive of the creator's computer.

Without incorporating intent into the concept of a record, everyone with a copy of the contract has a record—and, under most records policies, would need to retain it. This problem can be eliminated by stating in a policy that only the sender of an email or creator of a document is required to retain the record. Likewise, replies to email messages need to be retained only by those that compose and send the replies.

Clearly stating the organization's intent can create a clear chain of accountability and free up system resources.

Test Your Warrior Quotient: Are These Records?

- HTML documents containing advertisements for your company's products as seen on your company's business website

- An affirmative response to an email asking for the final go-ahead to execute a contract with a third party contractor

- Access log files that show who last entered doctor's orders into a patient's electronic medical record

- A vendor agreement to a change in project scope sent over the Internet and received on a PDA

- A voicemail recording from an auditor asking questions about documents required for an impending investigation

If you said, "all of these are records," you're right. The simple fact that information is created or stored electronically doesn't minimize its status as a business record. Don't be blindsided by the fact that digital information is easily disposable. Evaluate the importance of record content and retain the necessary information to meet your organization's business, compliance, operational, and legal needs.

Warriors with legal, RM, IT and business backgrounds can and should work together to determine what records they "intend" to retain for each new e-business process before it goes live.

Simplify Records Management Rules—Even Though Technology May be Complex

> *The ability to simplify means to eliminate the unnecessary so that the necessary may speak.*
>
> Hans Hofmann

When it comes to IMC, the most powerful and successful methods are often the simplest—because simple measures are easier to implement, easier to follow, and easier to manage.

If Warriors give in to the urge to overcomplicate IMC processes, they may cause a ripple effect that can further complicate other processes throughout the organization. Complexity now can lead to problems later, possibly resulting in noncompliance, business inefficiencies, or future legal problems.

Simplify, Simplify, Simplify

> *Everything should be made as simple as possible, but not simpler.*
>
> Albert Einstein

Warriors who are records managers live at the nexus of the organization's information assets. They spend most of their time handling the company's valued information as well as thinking about, classifying, and evaluating records materials and procedures.

If records managers design and implement complicated systems for processing the organization's information, they send the message that IMC is a complicated and daunting process. While instilling this view throughout the organization might ensure the records manager's job security, it will cause many problems, such as workers acting outside of normal procedures to avoid complications. Overburden employees with complex and time consuming processes and they'll likely begin to cut corners, not living up to the standards set in place.

As is often the case with internal service departments, Records Management is frequently required to do more with less. In smaller organizations, RM duties are often assigned to personnel that already have other full time responsibilities.

The RM Warrior's goal should be to simplify processes to make the job easier for everyone. One way that organizations could greatly benefit from simpler rules is in the area of retention. Yes, there are hundreds (or even thousands) of laws and regulations that may impact a large organization, and innumerable types of records, but if retention rules can't be simplified they will not be followed by employees, who are increasingly given responsibility for retention and disposal activities.

Automated Processes

Perhaps one of the most effective ways of simplifying records and information management practices is to automate them. Many IMC functions can be automated with the help of IT, such as:

- Controlling access to records
- Indexing, searching, and retrieving records
- Flagging and classifying emails
- Controlling the way employees access and use records information
- Providing computer-based training and testing
- Creating a workflow process for approval of policies, retention periods, and so on

Automation can help to take the guesswork out of IMC, ensuring that policies and standards are consistently implemented and enforced. Consider controlling electronic records centrally with software tools such as Electronic Content Management software. Let systems help control what employees can and cannot do with company e-records.

Where systems are not automated, make sure information and Records Management methods are practical—that they serve the organization's business and legal needs without overburdening staff or company systems.

Employee Education

Make IMC as simple and transparent as possible, but don't neglect to educate employees on their responsibilities. No matter how secure and stable your IMC systems, there will always be times when employees need to make informed decisions about how to handle the company's information. Don't make them guess. Work to generate awareness of IMC throughout the organization and make sure employees know who to contact with questions and how to contact them.

Provide a simple guide to information and records management requirements and processes in an easily accessible location, such as on the organization's Intranet website. Make it available to all employees, and update the guide as new questions arise.

Put a New Face on Records Management

31

Records Management may have gotten a bad rap in the past, but the time has never been better to improve its image.

The bespectacled paper pusher, carting away boxes of paper documents to a distant warehouse is a stereotype that's losing ground. The rapid pace of business and the enormous volumes of information passing through network systems call for a new breed of records manager who can corral massive amounts of information and produce it on demand. This is the role of the Warrior.

The Warrior knows how to effectively collect and store information for Records Management's internal customers, is able to produce information on demand for the business, and is able to anticipate what information will be needed and when.

The Warrior takes Records Management to the next level. All business units routinely rely on paper and digital information and many struggle with finding the right information at the right time. This provides the Warrior the opportunity to be the problem solver, helping to ensure that information is available whenever it is needed by whomever it is needed, and assisting with long-term management until disposition. The Warrior can change the RM image from one of passive records storage to one of active information management by offering training, generating awareness, and asking and answering questions throughout the organization.

Don't Be a Myopic "Expert"

In many fields, the "experts" who have mastered the discipline consistently underestimate the potential for that information to be misunderstood by others. RM information workers may likewise run the risk of assuming that frontline employees and leadership fully comprehend the fundamentals of IMC, when in fact the opposite may be true.

Warriors must recognize that not everyone shares their familiarity and passion for information management. Assume nothing: simplify policy, instructions, rules, and training and make them as intuitive as possible. Remember everyone already has a full time job, so ensure that employees can perform their IMC responsibilities in a short amount of time.

Reach Out to Internal Customers

Warriors who reach out to other departments will go a long way towards changing the image of the Records Management Department from one of a tactical necessity to one that solves business problems.

Think about it. When was the last time you heard someone from another department say, "Is there anything my department can do to make your job any easier?" That's a powerful way to make allies while proving the relevance of RM.

Warriors should constantly be examining how they can bring the benefit of RM and IMC to the entire organization, and ask questions such as:

- What can RM do for other departments that they haven't thought of yet?

- How can RM work with the technologists to apply Records and Information Management strategies to IT problems?

- Do employees have the information they need at their fingertips and what can RM do to help increase accessibility and information and knowledge sharing?

Simply showing an interest in the needs and activities of other departments can improve Records Management's relationships with those areas. RM will also become better equipped to provide new business solutions in the future. Regular interaction with the rest of the organization will put a face on Records Management and might get employees thinking of the company's information in terms of assets that need to be managed.

Records Retention: What is Reasonable?

In a recent court case, a water park had its retention decisions reviewed and attacked. The company purged certain records after completion of the previous season. The court reasoned that if an injury claim was going to be brought against the company, the individual claim could be brought for several years according to the statute of limitations in the state. If the record at issue was disposed before the statute of limitation was over, the court determined that such disposition was inherently unreasonable.

Not long ago an issue was raised in another court case about the reasonableness of having different retention periods for an accident report and the pictures of the accident. The pictures were retained for 20 years, but the reports for only 2 years. The plaintiff argued that such inconsistencies were because the reports were usually critical of the manufacturer while the pictures weren't. As the case focused more and more on the retention inconsistency, and turned more contentious, the manufacturer agreed to settle the case before the court had a chance to decide the issue. Again, reasonableness and consistency were key.

While you should **not** run out and change all your retention periods based on these cases, they do raise the issue about how courts may view retention in the electronic age. If contract records are retained by a company for 7 years following the termination of a contract, but email messages dealing with the same contract are "retained" for 60 days and disposed of by the IT purge of the system, is it likely that the courts might find that unreasonable?

Teach Your Organization That All Employees Share Records Management Responsibilities

A key part of the Warrior's responsibility is promoting a culture of IMC in their organization. Records Management must be viewed as the responsibility of **every** employee. Getting real involvement in Records Management from employees enterprise-wide requires building an awareness of why RM is important, how it can add value to the business, and what its effective implementation requires.

Why is employee involvement in RM important?

- Workers throughout the organization have different perspectives that can benefit RM and can identify problem areas that records managers may not be aware of. A broad base of contacts can help records managers develop knowledge that can lead to new solutions or projects.

- Good relationships with employees increases the likelihood of success. Earning the respect and trust of workers that makes them comfortable with relying on the Records Management Department can prevent miscommunications or workers operating outside the program—such as hiding "their" records in their office rather than sending them to the records room for fear they'll be lost.

- Having employees knowledgeable of RM practices makes it easier to meet legal demands and compliance needs. Keeping workers informed and on good terms with the RM department enables two-way communication and information sharing that is more effective at protecting the organization's interests than the records manager going it alone.

There will often be instances where information workers don't know what records are being created or where they're being kept. All employees need to be aware that what they're doing with company information can have an effect on the organization because records managers can't always be there looking over their shoulders.

There are situations where employees have stewardship over their own files with the only backups buried deep within a central server or on tape, requiring great expense of time and manpower for IT to dig them out. Warriors should know how their organization backs up information and how retrievable it is so that they can help employees manage the information accordingly.

If employees are responsible for backing up their own files, they need to know how to keep the files accurate, trustworthy, and reliable. For frontline employees this may mainly be a question of media. Are paper printouts unsuitable due to space limitations? Can optical media be stored in a way that will ensure its integrity? If records are stored outside the records department, are they classified and organized properly with uniform heading information to ensure easy retrieval by anyone in the organization?

To involve employees throughout the organization in Records Management, Warriors need to:

- Get executives inspired to help promote the IMC program.
- Meet with representatives from business units to discuss the IMC issues that affect them. Promote shared values by taking an interest in what internal customers do.
- Promote RM as a service and deliver those services that internal customers need and want.
- Involve internal customers to build support for new projects from the start.
- Take suggestions from internal customers seriously.
- Provide a clear vision of what RM can do and what needs to be done.
- Partner with departments to become part of the solution to business problems.

Don't Leave Storage Options to Untrained Employees

Storage of company data is too important to leave to chance. When employees are backing up their own data, they need to understand the limitations of the media they use.

Backup tapes will be rendered unreadable if demagnetized, as may be the case when they are left by a CRT monitor for extended periods of time.

Optical media such as CD-ROMs and DVDs can be damaged through improper storage or handling that may make the data unreadable.

Optical media can be damaged by environmental conditions such as extreme heat and dust. Optical media used for archival purposes may need to be stored vertically to prevent gravity from warping the disk.

Using labels on optical media can decrease their lifespan by trapping moisture on the surface of the disk. Disks can be safely labeled with a fine point permanent marker.

Use Records Management Expertise to Aid Business Continuity

The blackout that hit Ontario in August caused the Canadian economy to stumble badly, with Statistics Canada saying August GDP posted an even bigger monthly decline than the one caused by the extremist attacks of September 2001.

Canadian Broadcasting
Corporation News, October 2003[94]

In August 2003, a massive blackout left 50 million Americans and Canadians in the dark, spanning an area that covered eight U.S. states and Canada's most populous province of Ontario. The mammoth power failure took out major financial centers like New York City and Toronto, knocking both businesses and governments on their heels as billions of dollars circled the drain.[95]

Although most of the lights were back on in 24 hours, the U.S. Department of Energy estimates the total cost of the blackout to businesses, government, workers, and shareholders was over $6 billion.[96]

Companies suffer huge financial losses if their systems go down for even a single day, so designing an ironclad business continuity plan is a critical business imperative. Unfortunately, many organizations fail to cover all the bases, only considering the full range of risks after systems have been knocked out of commission.

Warriors should play a key role in their organization's disaster recovery plan. The expertise that Warriors have on classifying, retaining, and making critical information available is central to an organization's ability to reestablish their operations in the event of a disaster.

Records Management and Business Continuity are Not the Same Thing

> *If there's one thing . . . learned from the World Trade Center disaster it's that when it comes to data storage, recovery from a tape is about as efficient as swimming upstream.*
>
> Wall Street & Technology[97]

Records Management and the organization's business continuity efforts are two distinct processes that shouldn't overlap. Their priorities are different and they serve different ends.

- Records Management aims at making the most of the organization's information resources, dispensing with outdated material to cut costs, and ensuring the integrity and trustworthiness of company records.

- Business continuity efforts focus on managing information and infrastructure to prevent lost revenue and decreased customer satisfaction by keeping the business running when things don't go as planned.

Organizations should keep the distinct goals of each discipline in mind when setting up a Business Continuance framework.

But just because RM and business continuity should be treated as separate entities doesn't mean a business continuity program won't benefit from a meeting of the minds. Many IT departments do a great job addressing business continuity and potential disasters, but technologists aren't necessarily trained to be records managers.

Business Continuity Needs the RM Perspective

Dedicating a team of diverse professionals to address business continuity needs will help the organization focus on what needs to be done and how to do it, allowing the enterprise to leverage each department's specific knowledge and skills to protect business's processes and critical data. The bulk of the work should be performed *before* disaster strikes, by forecasting various threats that may put company information at risk and planning for various contingencies.

Warriors, especially those with RM expertise, can add valuable insight to a Business Continuance program team as they are responsible for the organization's information assets enterprise wide. This makes them well suited to address the business continuity needs of the total organization as well as the specific needs of individual units and departments.

While the IT department is proficient in getting systems up and running again quickly, the records manager is skilled in evaluating the value of various types of information and disaster recovery methods, ensuring mission critical records and information have the fastest recovery time possible and are restored to a trustworthy state. RM Warriors know where the records are and how long they must be retained; they are familiar with what information the organization needs to operate effectively; and they will likely know what data is non-critical and can be allowed a slower recovery time.

Disaster Recovery Checklist

- Are sufficient backup methods in place? Is the current backup schedule sufficient to protect the organization's critical information?

- Does the organization provide regular training, including practice drills, to parties responsible for recovering data to ensure recovery time objectives can easily be met?

- Is the Disaster Recovery Plan designed to protect the total organization yet sufficiently tailored to meet the needs of individual departments?

- Does the organization have a well-trained Disaster Recovery Team involving representatives from all departments?

- Is there a well-documented disaster recovery plan in place and does it have executive approval? Has the plan been distributed to the necessary people? Is the plan regularly updated to address business and infrastructure changes as well as new potential threats?

- Does the organization document and learn from past disasters? Does it consider events that have affected others in similar industries?

Harness Technology to Manage E-Records

"Thus the paradox in all this abundance is that the easier it is to create and store information, the harder that information is to manage, and the greater is the threat that we will not be able to find something when we need it. There is simply too much to sort through."

Deanna B. Marcum, *New York Times*[98]

The sheer volume of business information that must be managed today is overwhelming, and the problem is growing. So much so that entire families of technologies—including document management, email management, and records management—have been developed to facilitate the management of technology, or more specifically, to manage the output of IT: email messages, instant messages, electronic forms, spreadsheets, digital images, compressed log files, and so on.

Warriors need to use IT to take control of their digital information assets to ensure that e-records are accessible and useable to the business in a way that improves efficiency and contributes strategically.

Audit Trails

Computer generated audit trails are designed to independently record the time and date of all user actions—access, data entry, file modifications, and deletions. Time stamped records of these actions are stored in a secure database but can also attach themselves to the file's metadata. This happens automatically so that users cannot interfere with the process. The audit trail can be designed to log the system actions of all personnel, storing the data history in a form that can be viewed but is impossible to alter. The audit trail is a widely recognized method of security monitoring that provides a record of system events to establish a chain of accountability and may serve to bolster evidentiary value.

Audit trails can and perhaps should record the following:

- **System queries.** Who searched for what records or information, and when the search occurred.

- **Actions within a given time frame or on specific dates.** All system activities are dated with a time stamp for an accurate chronological record of events.

- **User activities.** Records all actions taken under a specific user ID and password combination.

- **Records histories.** Memorializes when specific records were accessed, viewed, printed, copied, modified, or deleted.

- **Terminal use.** Identifies which user acted from a specific workstation, what they used it for, and when.

What Can Audit Trails Be Used For?

- Who sends an email, what the content was, and when it was sent.

- Web transaction: When customers visited and left the site, what they did while they were on the site, the time and date of implementing an e-signature for a particular transaction, and the related terms and conditions that were applicable at the time of the signing.

- Who created a record and when it was created, printed, modified, or deleted.

Manage in Electronic Form

Digital business content often contains information that is lost or significantly altered when it is printed. Courts and rules of evidence have responded to these facts by allowing (and in some cases requiring) parties to a dispute to have access to digital "live" versions of electronic records, despite the fact that "complete" paper versions were already available.

In *Public Citizen v. John Carlin*,[99] the court asserted that records created electronically should remain in electronic form because there was information available in electronic form that was not available when printed to paper. They used the example of spreadsheet calculation to demonstrate the point. While the case was overturned for unrelated reasons, regulators may take the position that "once electronic, always electronic" is the only way to retain such records. Further, there are many business benefits to managing digital content in its original form, such as ease of searching, retrieval, integration, and dissemination.

Consequently, organizations should manage digital content in its original format whenever practical or required.

Proper E-Disposal: Cleansing Hard Drives

It is critical that organizations ensure the hard drives on all computers are thoroughly cleansed of internal information before machines are decommissioned or resold.

Even computer vendors are recognizing the risk—a well-known computer company recently announced a service plan that allows customers to retain their old hard drives when having them replaced or upgraded.[101] If a consumer products company is sensitized to these issues, clearly those responsible for managing corporate information need to be as well.

Computers Reveal the Clockwork Behind an Organization

Computer data can say a lot about the way an organization operates. Day-to-day business activities and operations, relationships between workers and departments, successes, failures, mistakes, and mishaps are all secreted away somewhere in the organization's network—even in the case of an organization as secretive and decentralized as a terrorist group.

A clever reporter on the ground in Afghanistan, during the U.S.-led war against the Taliban, sought out and purchased two computers stolen from Al Qaeda operatives in Kabul.[100] The hard drive of one of the computers revealed a wealth of information about how the terrorists operate. Email messages were found on the drive that described squabbles with local leaders, outlined the organization's high level strategies, and revealed codes used in electronic communications. Other messages revealed typical issues that must be addressed by any organization, such as tracking budget expenses, as in this outgoing message to a terrorist cell in Yemen:

"Why did you give out loans? Didn't I give clear orders to Muhammad Saleh...to refer any loan requests to me?"

"Why did you buy a new fax for $470? Where are the two old faxes? Did you get permission before buying a new fax under such circumstances?"

"Please explain the cellphone invoice amounting to $756 (2,800 riyals) when you have mentioned communication expenses of $300."

"Why are you renovating the computer? Have I been informed of this?"

A recent study of nearly 200 hard drives from used computers found medical records, love letters, pornography, and thousands of credit card numbers still stored on those drives.

Business data found included:[102]

- Software source code from high-tech companies
- Confidential memos
- Internal spreadsheets
- Company emails

- Financial information from an investment firm

- Transactions, account numbers, and withdrawal amounts from an ATM hard drive

- More than 5000 credit card numbers from a cash register hard drive

Many business and government organizations have been bitten by not adequately sanitizing discarded drives:

- The U.S. Veterans Administration gave away 139 computers containing veterans' medical records and 44 government credit card numbers to schools, state agencies, and thrift

Test Your Warrior Quotient: Decommissioning

The T. Julian hospital is about to decommission some older computers and wants to ensure that all sorts of medical records have been totally purged before being donated to the Red Chief Boys Club.

Which disposal method seems prudent?

1. Demanding that employees delete all the records, one by one to make sure each is gone.

2. Over-writing the hard drive according to Department of Defense standards.

3. Taking the hard drive out and destroying the units physically.

4. Selling it to LuLu's Second Chance Resale Shop and getting a certified letter that she has purged the contents.

Answer: Today, given changes in the law and the need for thorough disposal, options 2 or 3 are the best answers. Just because something is deleted does not mean it is really gone for good. #1 is not a good option because although the index reference is gone when a record is deleted, the content part is still on the hard drive until it is overwritten by new data. Whether or not Lulu gives you a certified letter that she did the purging properly may not relieve you of your responsibility to properly dispose of the contents. While destroying the hard drives may seem extreme and costly (rendering the computer useless without a new hard drive), some companies are now doing just that to ensure the content is gone forever.

stores. The undeleted patient information included the records of psychiatric and AIDS patients. An Indianapolis reporter discovered the blunder after purchasing three of the machines from a local thrift store.[103]

- An Internet consulting firm with prominent clients in the IT industry outsourced the sale of fewer than 100 computers, later hearing reports that confidential business information was still on some of the auctioned hard drives, despite contractual obligations to wipe the drives clean of all remaining data.[104]

Don't Forget Records Management Fundamentals in the Digital World

Warriors need to ensure that RM fundamentals are brought into the digital world—just because information is in digital form does not mean that the retention rules change. Although RM activities and challenges may be different in the digital world, the need to retain and manage records does not alter.

Even "Transitory" Records Need to Be Managed

Most electronic information comes into existence without prior thought as to how it will be identified, retained, protected, and made accessible in the future, when in fact such considerations should be an inherent part of any technology purchasing and implementation cycle. It is much easier and cheaper to build a new system correctly from the outset than to break old habits and modify an entrenched installation. In addition, employees should be trained to identify and manage business content that they generate directly and their conduct in this regard should be audited.

Identify What You Need to Retain and Access the Record

While the content of a paper document is obvious "on its face," viewing the contents of a digital document depends on software and hardware. Consequently, the proper indexing of digital content is fundamental to its utility. Without an index, retrieving digital information is expensive and time consuming, if it can be retrieved at all. In a recent case, a company could not search imaged medical claims records because the wrong metadata had been used in the indexing process, and they were therefore required to open and examine each record individually at great expense.

Pay Attention to Retention

Storing digital information without regard to content or future requirements is not a tenable approach to information management. While many organizations rely on backup tapes for storage of "mission-critical" data for disaster recovery purposes, they should not rely on these procedures for their information management retention needs.

Backup systems are generally designed to minimize the storage burden, not to enable easy retrieval of individual records. Consequently, the cost of information retrieval from backup systems can be very high. In one case, experts estimated the cost of reviewing email contained on twelve monthly backup sessions to be at least $99,000 and 660 labor hours.[105] In addition, the courts have been willing to impose arduous requirements on litigants to access stored electronic records. In *re Brand Name Prescription Drugs Antitrust Litigation*,[106] the court ordered one of the parties to develop a special computer program to extract data from nearly 30 million pages of email stored on backup tapes. Today, there are many cases where the costs associated with finding, unearthing, and producing e-information have exceeded $1,000,000.

Can You Find it and Access It?

Capturing and storing digital business content serves little purpose if it is not readily accessible when required. Too often organizations implement systems that may improve business processes but hamper the accessibility of significant business content, a fact that the courts and regulators may be unwilling to overlook.

In Florida, county officials admitted that they were violating the law by failing to produce requested e-records but asserted that it would take hundreds of hours and thousands of unbudgeted dollars to produce them. Instead, they "suggested that residents interested in public officials' email would need to sit at each official's computer and manually check the e mail received."[107]

Dispose of it Properly

Just like paper records, electronic records need to be disposed of at the end of their useful life in conformance with predefined retention rules. Proper disposition eases the information management burden by reducing storage volumes, making needed information more readily available, and controlling future management expenses. Organizations should ensure that disposition is done in the "ordinary course of business," and that documentary evidence is kept regarding the salient details of the disposition process (e.g., date of disposition, individual conducting disposition, and method of disposition). Storage media containing confidential and sensitive information must be thoroughly purged using appropriate techniques, such as those outlined by the U.S. Department of Defense *DoD 5220.22-M* standard,[108] to ensure that data cannot be recovered using advanced forensic techniques.

Endnotes

[1] "The Current State of Information Management Compliance: An Industry Study Conducted by AIIM International and Kahn Consulting, Inc., 2004."

[2] SEC Final Rule, "Management's Reports on Internal Control Over Financial Reporting and Certification of Disclosure in Exchange Act Periodic Reports," [RELEASE NOS. 33-8238; 34-47986; IC-26068; File Nos. S7-40-02; S7-06-03].

[3] COBIT Framework, 3rd Edition, COBIT Steering Committee and the IT Governance Institute, July 2000.

[4] COSO Framework - Information and Communication.

[5] Rambus, Inc. v. Infineon Techs. AG, 220 F.R.D. 264.

[6] SEC Release No. 49386, March 10, 2004.

[7] Adapted from, Kahn, Randolph A., and Barclay T. Blair, Information Nation: Seven Keys to Information Management Compliance, AIIM Publications, 2004, 69-70.

[8] *Anti-Monopoly, Inc. v. Hasbro, Inc.,* 1995 WL 649934 (SDNY, 1995).

[9] "Web Mishap: Kids' Psychological Files Posted," *Los Angeles Times,* November 7, 2001.

[10] Zack, Ian, "Lawsuit Puts Customer Service On Notice," Forbes.com, February 1, 2002.

[11] *People v. Superior Court,* 2004 WL 1468698 (Cal. Ct. App. June 29, 2004).

[12] *Campbell v. General Dynamics Gov't Sys. Corp.,* 321 F.Supp.2d 142 (D.Mass 2004).

[13] *AFD Fund v. United States,* 61 Fed. Cl. 540 (Fed. Cl. 2004).

[14] *State v. Voorheis,* 844 A.2d 794 (Vt. 2004).

[15] Canada Evidence Act, Section 31.5 states: "For the purpose of determining under any rule of law whether an electronic document is admissible, evidence may be presented in respect of any standard, procedure, usage or practice concerning the manner in which electronic documents are to be recorded or stored, having regard to the type of business, enterprise or endeavour that used, recorded or stored the electronic document and the nature and purpose of the electronic document."

[16] *Zubulake v. UBS Warburg*, LLC, CIV.02-1243, 2003 WL 21087884 (S.D.N.Y. May 13, 2003).

[17] "Forensic Examination of Digital Evidence: A Guide for Law Enforcement," U.S. Department of Justice Office of Justice Programs, April 2004.

[18] COBIT Framework, 3rd Edition, COBIT Steering Committee and the IT Governance Institute, July 2000.

[19] The Sedona Principles: "Best Practices Recommendations & Principles for Addressing Electronic Document Production," A Project of The Sedona Conference Working Group on Best Practices for Electronic Document Retention & Production, January 2004.

[20] "Managing Complexity," *The Economist*, November 17, 2004, pp 71–73.

[21] "Accenture Welfare Payment System Under Fire in Ontario," Marc Songini, *Computerworld*, July 29, 2004.

[22] United States General Accounting Office, "National Archives and Records Administration's Acquisition of Major System Faces Risks," *GAO Highlights*, August 2003.

[23] The Project Management Institute (www.pmi.org) is one organization that offers project management certification.

[24] Bruce Gilchrist and Milton R. Wessel, "Government Regulation of the Computer Industry," AFIPS Press, New Jersey, February 1972.

[25] *Cobell v. Norton*, 274 F. Supp. 2d 111, 116 (D.D.C., 2003).

[26] DiSabatino, Jennifer, "Court Order Shuts Down Dept. of Interior Web Sites," *Computerworld,* Dec. 17, 2001.

[27] Inouye, Daniel, "Statement of Senator Daniel K. Inouye, Chairman, Committee on Indian Affairs, Before the July 25, 2002 Hearing on The Report of the Department of the Interior Submitted to the Congress on July 2, 2002 on the Historical Accounting of Individual Indian Money Accounts," Jul. 25, 2002.

[28] *Cobell v. Norton,* 274 F. Supp. 2d 111 (D.D.C., 2003)

[29] California Senate Bill 1386, February 12, 2002.

[30] "Recent Court Ruling in Cobell Case Leaves BIA Schools Without Internet Access," Mar. 19, 2004, Online at http://daschle.senate.gov/~daschle/pressroom/ releases/04/03/2004319508.html

[31] "Tower Records Settles FTC Charges," Federal Trade Commission, Apr. 21, 2004.

[32] Ibid.

[33] Ibid.

[34] Lyman, Peter, and Hal R. Varian. "How Much Information?" Berkeley, CA: University of California-Berkeley School of Information Management and Science, 2003.

[35] "VoIP/IP Telephony Statistics," *Commweb,* Oct. 15, 2002.

[36] *Vonage Holdings Corp. v. Minn. PUC,* 290 F. Supp. 2d 993 (D. Minn., 2003).

[37] Royalty, Paula K., "When is a Phone Call Not a Phone Call? Legal Issues Arising From Business Use of VoIP," *Shidler Journal of Law, Commerce and Technology,* May 26, 2004.

[38] Kentucky Cent. Life Ins. Co. v. Jones, 1993 U.S. App. LEXIS 21976 (6th Cir., 1993).

[39] Ibid.

[40] Joe Jakubowski. "Protecting the Heart of the Desktop," *Storage Network World Online*, May 27, 2003.

[41] *Rambus, Inc. v. Infineon Techs.* AG, 220 F.R.D. 264.

[42] *Keir v. UnumProvident Corp.*, 2003 U.S. Dist. LEXIS 14522 (D.N.Y., 2003).

[43] *Applied Telematics v. Sprint Communs.* Co., L.P., 1996 U.S. Dist. LEXIS 14053 (D. Pa., 1996).

[44] *Mathias v. Jacobs*, 197 F.R.D. 29; 2000 U.S. Dist. LEXIS 10547 (S.D.N.Y. 2000).

[45] *Bills v. Kennecott Corp.*, 108 F.R.D. 459, 462 (D. Utah 1985).

[46] SEC Release No. 49386, March 10, 2004.

[47] *Positive Software Solutions, Inc. v. New Century Mortg. Corp.*, 2003 U.S. Dist. LEXIS 7659 (N.D. Tex. May 2, 2003).

[48] FCC Third Order and Report, 2000.

[49] UETA § Section 7.

[50] Public Law 106-229.

[51] "Retention Of Electronic Records; Originals," UETA Section 12.

[52] *M.A. Mortenson Co. v. Timberline Software Corp.*, 140 Wn.2d 568 (Wash., 2000).

[53] Eric Nee, "SOX in a Box: Due Diligence," CIO Insight, May 1, 2004.

[54] CNN Money, "China executes bank staff for fraud," Sep. 14, 2004.

[55] SEC Release No. 33-8230, "Mandated Electronic Filing and Website Posting for Forms 3, 4, and 5," May 7, 2003.

[56] "The Current State of Information Management Compliance: An Industry Study Conducted by AIIM International and Kahn Consulting, Inc., 2004."

[57] *Jasmine Networks, Inc. v. Marvell Semiconductor, Inc.,* 117 Cal. App. 4th 794 (Cal. Ct. App., 2004).

[58] Radicati Group, as quoted by John Dickinson, "Radicati Forecasts Huge Growth For Enterprise IM," *InternetWeek,* July 15, 2004.

[59] "Email Policies and Practices: An Industry Study Conducted by AIIM International and Kahn Consulting, Inc., 2003."

[60] "Financial Institution Letters: Guidance on Instant Messaging," FIL-84-2004, FDIC, Jul. 21, 2004.

[61] Osterman, Michael, "IM a wiretapper," *Network World Messaging Newsletter,* April 27, 2004.

[62] *State ex rel. Dispatch Printing Co. v. City of Columbus,* 90 Ohio St. 3d 39 (Ohio, 2000).

[63] *In re Prudential Ins. Co. of Am. Sales Practices Litig.,* 169 F.R.D. 598 (D.N.J., 1997).

[64] Ibid.

[65] "Arthur Andersen Found Guilty of Obstructing Justice," *Washington Post,* Jun. 15, 2002.

[66] Manor, Robert, "Without audit practice, not much left," *Chicago Tribune,* Jun. 17, 2002,

[67] Dey, Iain, "Ex SEC chairman to monitor WorldCom," *The Scotsman,* Jul. 4, 2002.

[68] Evers, Joris, "Monitor appointed in WorldCom case, trial in March," *Computerworld,* Jul. 5, 2002.

[69] Ibid.

[70] Jewell, Mark, "Federal agents serve warrants at ITT Technical Institute campuses in records probe," Associated Press, February 25, 2004.

[71] CNN/Money, "Fraud charges sink education stocks," June 24, 2004.

[72] Ibid.

[73] *Convolve, Inc. v. Compaq Computer Corp.,* 223 F.R.D. 162, 177 (D.N.Y., 2004).

[74] *Zubulake v. UBS Warburg LLC,* 2004 U.S. Dist. LEXIS 3574 (D.N.Y., 2004)

[75] Hazelton, Peter M., "California privacy laws could impact Ohio businesses," BizJournals.com, April 16, 2004.

[76] SB 1386, February 12, 2002.

[77] Sine, Richard, "Second Anniversary: The Impact of Sarbanes-Oxley," *The Friday Report* (Institutional Shareholder Services) 2004.

[78] Ibid.

[79] Tim Greene, "IT staffs use fear to sell security," *Network World,* 10/26/04.

[80] "IT budgets hit by compliance costs: CBI says new rules are stifling UK finance firms," James Watson and Miya Knights, *Computing,* 27 Oct 2004.

[81] "Growth at McKinsey Hindered Use of Data," *Wall Street Journal,* May 20, 2002.

[82] "The Struggle To Align IT With Business Goals: The Mercury Interactive IT Executive Survey," A Study Conducted By Forrester Research, 2003.

[83] Ibid.

[84] Capaccio, Tony, "Boeing target of U.S. inquiry," *Seattle Post Intelligencer,* July 28, 2001.

[85] Lichtblau, Eric, "F.B.I. Said to Lag on Translating Terror Tapes," *New York Times,* Sep. 27 2004.

[86] Kehaulani Goo, Sara, "Controllers' 9/11 Tape Destroyed, Report Says," *Washington Post,* May 7, 2004.

[87] Ibid.

[88] *Lewy v. Remington Arms Co.*, 836 F.2d 1104 (8th Cir., 1988).

[89] Ibid.

[90] Dunn, John E., "Trojan Spams Russian Mobile Phones," Techworld.com, November 10, 2004.

[91] Mintz, John and Abse, Nathan, "Glitches Altered Version of Starr Report Online," *Washington Post,* September 16, 1998.

[92] Rugman, Jonathan, "Downing St dossier plagiarized," Channel 4 News online, Feb. 6, 2003.

[93] Thibodeau, Kenneth, "Preservation and Migration of Electronic Records: The State of the Issue," U.S. National Archives and Records Administration, September 2, 2004.

[94] "August blackout leads to big drop in GDP," CBC.ca news, Oct. 31, 2003.

[95] "The Economic Impacts of the August 2003 Blackout," Electricity Consumers Resource Council, Feb. 9, 2004.

[96] Glotfelty, Jim, "Transforming the Grid to Revolutionize Electric Power in North America," U.S. Department of Energy, Jan. 27 2004.

[97] Middlemiss, Jim, "Running Out of Room: Data-Storage Needs Explode," *Wall Street & Technology,* Nov 11, 2002.

[98] Marcum, We Can't Save Everything, *New York Times* (Op/Ed), July 6, 1998.

[99] *Public Citizen v. John Carlin*, 1997 U.S. Dist. Lexis 16993 (D.D.C. 1997).

[100] Cullison, Alan, "Inside Al-Qaeda's Hard Drive: Budget squabbles, baby pictures, office rivalries—and the path to 9/11," *Atlantic Monthly,* Sep. 2004.

[101] Burt, Jeffrey, "Gateway Lets Buyers Keep Old Hard Drives," *EWeek,* August 23, 2004.

[102] Garfinkel, Simson, "Hard-Disk Risk: Are all those old hard drives you're getting rid of free of important company data? Don't be so sure," *CSO Magazine,* April 2003.

[103] Hasson, Judi, "VA toughens security after PC disposal blunders," *Federal Computer Week,* 26 August, 2o02.

[104] Lyman, Jay, "Troubled Dot-Coms May Expose Confidential Client Data," Newsfactor.com, August 8, 2001.

[105] Aragon, Lawrence, "E-Mail is Not beyond the Law," *PC Week,* October 6, 1997.

[106] 123 F.3d 599, 609(7th Cir. 1997).

[107] "County Can't Deliver Email to Public," *St. Petersburg Times,* September 19, 2000.

[108] DoD 5220.22-M, otherwise known as the "National Industrial Security Program Operating Manual (NISPOM)."

Index

9/11, 167, 175

ABA, *See* American Bar Association

access controls, 23, 30, 95

access logs, 15, 181–82, 183

AFD Fund v. United States, 47

Afghanistan, 204

Al Qaeda, 167, 204

American Bar Association, 54

Andersen, *See* Arthur Andersen

application service providers, 61

Arthur Andersen, 96, 129, 140

ASP, *See* application service provider

attorney-client privilege, 103

audit trails, 15, 23, 116, 181–82, 201–2

backup media, 89, 99, 195

   See also storage media

backups, 4, 42, 80, 105, 132, 200

backup systems, 3, 25, 32, 37, 94, 194, 208

best practices, 49, 50–51, , 52–53, 54, 66

BIA, *See* Bureau of Indian Affairs (U.S.)

blogs, 25, 125

Brand Name Prescription Drugs Antitrust Litigation, 208

Bureau of Indian Affairs (U.S.), 81

business continuity, 197, 198, 199

   See also disaster recovery

calendaring, online, 156

California Database Protection Act, 80, 117, 133, 138

Campbell v. General Dynamics Gov't Sys. Corp, 47

Canada Standards Act, 50

Carlin, John, *See* Public Citizen v. John Carlin

case law, 47, 52, 160

   See also name of specific case

cell phones, *See* mobile devices

certification, 31, 51, 68, 116

champion (for IMC), 13, 16, 145, 149–51, 172

change management, 13, 69, 159–60

Civil Discovery Standards, 54

classification of information, 38, 39, 40, 115, 155, 186, 187, 194, 207

click-through agreements, *See* click wrap agreements

click-wrap agreements, 1–2, 43, 110–12

Cobell v. Norton, 79, 81
COBIT Framework, 32–33, 54
Committee of Sponsoring Organizations of the Treadway
    Commission, *See* COSO Framework
communications to employees, 38, 47, 52, 69, 102, 103, 131, 160
computers, decommissioning, 23, 203–6
confidential information, 23, 26, 40, 42, 111, 157, 204, 206, 209
    See also privacy
content, structured, 54
content, unstructured, 102
content management, 6, 45–46
Control Objectives for Information and Related Technology,
    See COBIT Framework
corporate governance, 138, 163–64
COSO Framework, 33
CRM, *See* customer relationship management systems
customer relationship management systems, ix, 46, 56, 144, 157–58
customer service (internal), 190–91
D. Chance Fabrics Manufacturer, 36
database systems, 46, 47, 57, 90, 153, 201–2
data management, 32, 54
delegation, 9
Department of Defense (U.S.), 209
Department of Education (U.S.), 130
Department of Energy (U.S.), 197
Department of Justice (U.S.), 54
Department of the Interior (U.S.), 79
destruction of evidence, 127–28, 129, 176–77
    See also records, destruction
digital information, *See* electronic records; *See* email
digital rights management, 86
disaster recovery, 41, 197, 200
    See also business continuity
discovery, *See* electronic discovery
document management (systems), 57, 144, 201
DOD, *See* Department of Defense (U.S.)
DOI, *See* Department of the Interior (U.S.)
DOJ, *See* Department of Justice (U.S.)
DRM, *See* digital rights management
electronic discovery
    back-up tapes, 35
    costs, 10, 59–60, 208
    court rulings, 52
    readiness assessment, 93–97
    requirements, 101
    responsiveness, 96

tactical approach, 71, 74

types of, 56–57, 201

information technology, See also specific types

infrastructure (IT), 56

instant messaging, 10, 47, 84, 92, 121–24, 123, 125

intelligence information, 10

intent, 91, 182–83

Interactive Voice Response, 40

internal controls, 29–31, 32–35, 54, 134

International Organization for Standardization, 54

ISO, *See* International Organization for Standardization

IT, *See* information technology

IT department, 71–72, 73–7

IVR, *See* Interactive Voice Response

Justice Department (U.S.), 164

knowledge management, 155–56

laptops, *See* mobile devices

laws, *See* name of specific law

legal hold, 4, 94, 96–97, 101–3, 104, 120, 131–32

letter of the law, 80

lifecycle of information, 87–90

litigation preparation, 38

low hanging fruit, 170

Lushco, 36

management by objectives, 143–44

metadata, 36, 40, 178–80, 207

Microfilm and Electronic Images as Documentary Evidence, 50

Minnesota Public Utilities Commission, 83

mobile devices, 26–27, 26, 57, 85, 124, 178

NARA, *See* National Archives and Administration (U.S.)

NASC, *See* National Association of Securities Dealers

National Archives and Administration (U.S.), 65

National Association of Securities Dealers, 123

Norton, *See* Cobell v. ...

Ontario Ministry of Community and Social Services (Canada), 63

optical disks, *See* storage media

organizational change, 6–7, 138, 158

outsourcing, 61

patch management, 21, 23, 31, 41, 124

penalties, 3, 7, 25, 36, 44, 59, 81, 82, 95, 105, 114, 117, 128–29, 164, 176

People's Republic of China, 114

People v. Superior Court, 47

pilot projects, 63

policies and procedures, 4, 24–25, 38, 39, 40, 52–53, 82–83, 122, 128

interdependent roles, 4

IT Warrior, 11

Legal Department, 102

Legal Warrior, 12

Records Management Warrior, 13–14

suppliers, 94

warriors, 9

retention, *See* records retention

return on investment, 58–59

RFP, *See* request for proposal

RM, *See* records management

ROI, *See* return on investment

sanctions, *See* penalties

Sarbanes-Oxley Act, 29, 31, 32, 46, 75, 86, 115–16, 117, 134, 137, 138, 163, 164

scope creep, 67, 68

SEC, *See* Securities and Exchange Commission (U.S.)

Securities and Exchange Commission (U.S.), 80, 104, 123, 129, 130, 164

security, 10, 25, 26, 41–42, 54, 79, 81, 82, 123

　See also encryption; *See also* patch management

Sedona Principles, 54

self assessment, 15-17

service level agreements, 22

service providers, 23, 94, 208

shrink-wrap agreements, 112

Six Sigma, 162

slamming, 107

software, *See* information technology

SOX, *See* Sarbanes-Oxley Act

spam, 23, 178

spirit of the law, 80

SSP, *See* storage service provider

standards, 50–51, 52–53, 54

State v. Voorheis, 47

storage media, 194, 195, 203, 209

storage service providers, 61

structured content, 57

Superior Court, *See* People v. ...

system design, compliance issues, 44, 48

system management, compliance issues, 48

Taliban, 204

TCF, *See* total cost of failure

TCO, *See* total cost of ownership

technology neutral regulations, 108, 117

telecommunications regulations, 83, 107

Kahn Consulting, Inc.
157 Leonard Wood North
Highland Park, IL 60035
847-266-0722
www.KahnConsultingInc.com

Kahn Consulting, Inc. ("KCI"), is a consulting firm specializing in the legal, compliance, and policy issues of information technology and information management. Through a range of services including information management compliance program development, risk management audits, policy development and evaluation, product assessments, legal and compliance research, and education and training, KCI helps its clients address today's critical issues in an ever-changing regulatory and technological environment. Based in Chicago, KCI provides its services to Fortune 500 companies and state and federal governmental agencies in North America and around the world.

AIIM

The Enterprise Content Management Association
About AIIM – The ECM Association

AIIM Headquarters
1100 Wayne Avenue, Suite 1100
Silver Spring, Maryland, US 20910
Phone: 800.477.2446 or 301.587.8202
Fax: 301.587.2711
E-mail: aiim@aiim.org
www.aiim.org

European Office

The IT Centre, 8 Canalside
Lowesmoor Wharf, Worcester
United Kingdom WR1 2RR
Phone: +44 (0) 1905.727.600
Fax: +44 (0) 1905.727.609
www.aiim.org.uk

For over 60 years, AIIM has been the leading international non-profit organization helping users understand the challenges associated with managing documents, content, and business processes. AIIM's core values reflect this long-term perspective:

- **International**—Members in over 75 countries

- **Independent**—Unbiased and vendor neutral

- **Implementation Focused**—Processes, not just technology

- **Industry Intermediary**—Users, suppliers, consultants, analysts, and the channel

AIIM defines Enterprise Content Management (ECM) as the technologies used to capture, manage, store, preserve, and deliver content and documents related to organizational processes. The ECM industry provides information management solutions to help users:

- Guarantee business **CONTINUITY**, 24x7x365

- Enable employee, partner, and customer **COLLABORATION**

- Ensure legal and regulatory **COMPLIANCE**

- Reduce **COSTS** through process streamlining and standardization

Get connected to the AIIM community, and see how AIIM can help you advance your professional career and grow your business. Visit us on the web at www.aiim.org.

MARKET EDUCATION—AIIM provides events and information services that help users specify, select, and deploy ECM solutions to solve organizational problems.

- *AIIM E-DOC Magazine*
  AIIM's bi-monthly flagship print publication reaches over 30,000 readers an issue with intelligent articles, case studies, thought-provoking columns, and lessons learned.

- ***M-iD* Magazine (Managing Information and Documents)**
  This leading publication, read by thousands of document management professionals in the United Kingdom, focuses specifically on the needs of those individuals responsible for the capture, storage and preservation, management, processing and delivery of information and documents.

- **Wednesday Webinar Series**
  No need to leave your office to attend a Wednesday Webinar. Each online presentation is FREE, and given by an industry expert, analyst, or author, and focuses on a specific ECM related issue each month.

- **Content Management Solutions Seminars**
  This FREE Seminar Series travels to 20 cities throughout the US and Canada and helps to educate thousands of end-users on the latest ECM technologies, critical implementation issues, and allows them to meet one-on-one with the experts.

- **Service Company Executive Forum**
  This exclusive meeting (in its 30th year) is being held November 10–12, 2005 in San Antonio, TX. It provides a unique opportunity for senior level service company executives, VARs, VADs, and systems integrators to come together and network with peers, discuss current and future business challenges, share experiences and strengthen business relationships.

- **Online Solution Centers**
  Join hundreds of AIIM web visitors at an AIIM Online Solution Center. Get focused articles, presentations, research studies, and more, for the Financial Services and Healthcare industry and Federal/State/Local Government.

- **Wall Posters**
  Thousands of office walls have been plastered with our wall posters. Help educate yourself and your colleagues on the lifecycle of ECM and Records Management.

- **IMExpo**
  This FREE event travels to 5 cities in the UK, and is dedicated to enterprise content management. The event offers a plethora of presentations, exhibits, and resources to help you tackle the projects to support your business processes, and raise the performance of your organization.

- **Info Ireland**
  Ireland's only dedicated two-day event for Information Management reaches hundreds of industry professionals. Tackle the issues connected to the management of documents, records and content, through briefings, discussions, and industry networking.

PROFESSIONAL DEVELOPMENT—AIIM provides an educational roadmap for the industry through online educational programs that help end users and suppliers learn more about the ECM industry.

- **ECM Certificate Program**
  This intensive, web-based certificate program contains two levels of education that provide a clear roadmap for industry professionals looking to expand their professional development and awareness of

ECM technologies. Learn the "Fundamentals" in Level 1, then, get the "Building Blocks" in Level 2.

- **IM University (UK)**
AIIM Europe's suite of dedicated expert-led education programs include a four day intensive program as well as a number of one day classroom based programs. IMUniversity also offers webinars—one off web-based lectures from industry figures—and a series of online lessons that cover all the fundamental aspects of ECM.

- **AIIM Annual Conference & Expo**
Produced by Advanstar Communications in cooperation with AIIM, this three-day networking and educational event for the ECM industry offers real solutions for business professionals seeking the latest technologies to develop, capture, manage, and store documents, information, and digital content to support business processes, comply with governmental regulations, drive down costs, and gain a competitive advantage.

- **ChannelConnection**
VARs, systems integrators, and service company professionals have one source for education, news, and resources to reach vendors and buyers of document management products and services.

INDUSTRY ADVOCACY—AIIM is the voice of the ECM industry in key standards organizations, with the media, and with government decision-makers. As an accredited American National Standards Institute (ANSI) development organization, AIIM plays an essential role in creating national and international standards, technical reports, surveys and recommended practices dealing with document and content management.

- **Committees**
Industry professionals dedicate their time to the growth and advancement of the document management industry as well as increasing their own expertise to develop AIIM standards and AIIM programs. Join a committee today that will shape the way the ECM industry grows.

- **Industry Watch Surveys and Analysis**
Several times a year, AIIM polls its end-user community for information about the ECM industry and shares the results with the membership.

PEER NETWORKING—AIIM chapters, programs, and our Web site create opportunities that expand the international base of users seeking ECM solutions and allow users, suppliers, and channel members to engage and connect with one another.

- **Communities**
Join an AIIM community and get connected with your peers in the ECM industry. Online or in person, these groups help to build your industry knowledge, connect with others in the industry, and increase awareness of the need for document management products in the business world.

- **39 Local Chapters**
Broaden your network and knowledge base, build business and personal relationships, and keep abreast of new technologies and products when you become involved in a local chapter.

MEMBERSHIP—Through year-round support, AIIM offers five types of membership to suit your needs. Pick the one that's best for you and become a recognized leader in the ECM industry; increase visibility for your company's products and services; develop standards for the industry; get news, information, and education; and network with industry professionals and peers.

- **Associate Membership (Users)**
Access to online content, DOC.1 enewsletter, *AIIM E-DOC Magazine*, and special events.

- **Professional Membership (Users)**
Access to members-only content, ECM Toolkit, committees, awards, and discounts on education and tools.

- **Trade Membership (Suppliers)**
Comprehensive market exposure through event and program sponsorships

- **Advisory Trade Membership (Suppliers)**
Representation on the AIIM Board of Directors plus maximum exposure and exclusive sponsorship discounts.

- **Channel Membership (Resellers, Distributors, and Service Providers)**
Specialized training, company visibility, education, and networking.

**Access Sciences
Corporation**

4710 Bellaire Blvd.
Suite 140
Bellaire, Texas 77401
800-242-2005
info@accesssciences.com
www.accesssciences.com

**Information Management Compliance Strategists
and Service Providers**

Access Sciences is a consulting and outsourcing firm providing leadership and expertise in the design, implementation, and maintenance of Information Management Compliance (IMC) programs. We lead and support IMC programs by developing strategies, establishing policies and work processes, creating retention schedules and file plans, evaluating and recommending software options, and operating and maintaining record centers and document control functions.

We applaud the key messages of *Information Nation Warrior* and underscore the value of systematic planning for Information Management Compliance. Access Sciences is a unique independent service provider well qualified to guide even the most complex Information Management programs. Our approach and methodologies are consistent with those conveyed so clearly in the *Information Nation* books written by these authors. As you consider your path forward, Access Sciences wants to be your trusted advisor.

Your Information is Our Business!

Our core business is providing Information Management consulting and outsourcing—from the local level to the global enterprise. For more than 20 years, Access Sciences has served customers ranging in size from Fortune 100® companies and large government agencies to small businesses and municipal entities.

Access Sciences consultants are records and content management experts with extensive real-world experience in a variety of industry settings. We deliver value to clients by offering a two-tier portfolio of services:

- *Consulting.* Our experienced professional consultants will assist your management team with every aspect of strategic planning, design, and implementation of a comprehensive and compliant Information Management program.
- *Outsourcing and Facility Operations.* We provide highly qualified professional project managers, records management staff, and skilled technical specialists to manage project teams or operate your information management facilities.

Access Sciences has demonstrated expertise in the following Enterprise Content Management and Compliance activities:

- Content management strategy—design, development, and implementation
- Best practices for life-cycle management of records and documents
- Best practices for Sarbanes-Oxley, HIPAA, GLB, and regulatory compliance
- Professional project management
- Workflow and process improvement
- Retention schedules, taxonomies, and filing plans
- Evaluation and implementation of content management technologies
- Information management outsourcing
- Imaging and document conversion
- Engineering document control
- Communication, training, and change management

Typical Outcomes and Benefits

- Improved organizational awareness and capability
- Enhanced collaboration and decision quality
- Faster access to key data
- Tighter data security
- Optimized record storage costs
- Minimized litigation risk
- Reduced discovery costs

How can Access Sciences help you?

Access Sciences would like to connect with you. Let our team of seasoned professionals guide and support your IMC and enterprise content management initiatives, and your ongoing information management program. Call us at (800) 242-2005, or visit us at www.accesssciences.com.

Captaris

The Way Information Moves

10885 NE 4th Street,
Suite 400
Bellevue, WA 98004
Phone: 425.455.6000
Fax: 425.638.1500
www.captaris.com

When do you need Captaris?

- When you need to automate business processes that involve document management and delivery,
- And you want to integrate the processes and data with your enterprise applications,
- Where fax and paper documents are involved,
- And you need to comply with regulations,
- And you love to grow revenues, increase profits and cut costs.
- Then it's time to call Captaris! We can help you.

Captaris is in the business of automating the information & document flow within organizations of any size throughout the information lifecycle (capture—process—archive—deliver). Our software solutions help organizations in every industry to grow revenue and cash, cut costs and meet compliance goals. Captaris has installed more than 90,000 systems in 95 countries in companies of all sizes, including the entire Fortune 100®.

With our comprehensive product suite and worldwide partner channel, we can deliver fast ROI solutions for any budget and any size enterprise in any country. We come from a very strong business information delivery (BID) heritage; in fact we're the worldwide market share leader in electronic fax document solutions.

Benefits of Working with Captaris

1. Single Source
2. Designed for fast ROI and compliance
3. World leader in business information delivery

We are the *single source* for key information and document flow technologies: workflow, fax servers, document management, records management and information delivery. Captaris owns and develops world-class technologies in business process workflow, fax servers, document and records management, and information delivery. Our customers enjoy the benefits of working with a single vendor.

We deliver solutions with *fast ROI* that drive revenue and cash growth, increased profitability and compliance for our customers. Our products are developed specifically for fast ROI. They are easy to install and test, require low resources for deployment and maintenance, and are engineered for maximum usability by office workers and executives alike. And because we own the key technologies, we can deliver better prices to our customers. The lower the 'I,' the faster the 'R.'

We've proven ourselves as the undisputed worldwide leader in BID solutions. Our RightFax product is the category leader in fax servers. Our Alchemy product is trusted for some of the world's most demanding information delivery applications.

The Product Line

We make software solutions that cover everything you need from beginning to end.

- Electronic fax servers to securely capture documents and replace fax machines.
- Document management software to capture all other documents and replace file cabinets.
- Workflow software to automate processes and shorten time-frames to completion.
- Enterprise integration software to connect with databases, ERP, CRM—whatever runs your business
- Archiving and records management software for compliance.
- Information delivery software to deliver the documents anywhere, anytime and on-time.

Customer Evidence

"Captaris Workflow really helped our business process because we had to map it. When it helps us to minimize risk and it costs a small fraction of the potential liability to do the project, that's a no-brainer."
　　　—CIO of a large CPA firm

"We chose MailStore because it enabled us to quickly meet the strict guidelines outlined in the SEC regulations. There are currently multiple solutions in the marketplace that would have met our compliance objective, but they were too expensive and required high-priced 'extras' to work effectively."
　　　—IT director for a brokerage firm

"Alchemy provided a simple index for any critical paperwork and efficiently manages retention policies according to compliance regulations."
　　　—IT director for an insurance services firm

"RightFax just out of the box is HIPAA-compliant."
　　　—IT coordinator for a large pharmacy services provider

Visit us at www.captaris.com

Eastman Kodak Company

Eastman Kodak Company
343 State Street
Rochester, NY 14650-1181
800-944-6171
dpsteam@kodak.com
www.kodak.com/go/docimaging
Infoimaging@Kodak

For more than 77 years, Kodak has empowered information processes with imaging. The resulting information exchange is called infoimaging, and it's the lifeblood of commercial and government organizations worldwide. Analyzing information provides the insights necessary to manage risk, minimize operational costs and optimize interactions with partners, supply chains and customers.

Infoimaging is a $385 billion industry created by the convergence of information technology and imaging science. And, Kodak is at the heart of it. In recent years, infoimaging has become increasingly important as many business processes have gone digital. The synergy of pictures coupled with information strikes a perfect balance between people and technology.

Data goes only so far. To complete the big picture, you require access to formatted documents and a variety of pictorial information. That's where Kodak's infoimaging solutions come in. Always responsive to the needs of its customers, Kodak has continued to develop products and product lines that make it easier for businesses of all sizes to better capture, manage, and deliver critical business information.

Who better than Kodak for Infoimaging?

Kodak delivers the broadest portfolio of products and services. We have the resources and tools to help you envision the possibilities—and potential—offered through the marriage of image science and information technology. We continually invest R&D into new products and product platforms across all categories in our portfolio.

If you use images, chances are we can streamline your processes with one or more of our technologies. If you market image-enabled products or services, we may be able to advance your time to market and improve your competitive position with hardware, enabling software and processing technologies.

Derive more value from your information with Kodak's imaging products

We enable images as a part of workflows and information repositories. In turn, this can heighten your abilities to automate process workflows, access information quickly, detect changes readily and communicate efficiently.

At Kodak, we have the people, processes and technology to significantly amplify how you use your information. To start putting imaging to work for you, call us at 800-944-6171 and request a copy of A-6313 (Introduction to Document Imaging) or A-6314 (Image Capture and Quality Issues). You can also visit us online at www.kodak.com/go/docimaging

FileNet Corporation

3565 Harbor Blvd.
Costa Mesa, CA 92626-1420
800-FileNet (345-3638 / 714-327-3400)
International: 714-327-4800
www.filenet.com

≢ _FILENET_®

In today's marketplace, ensuring regulatory compliance and good corporate governance has become a critical—and increasingly costly—business challenge. It is made more complex by the changeable nature of compliance itself and the fact that compliance today by no means ensures compliance tomorrow.

As a result, many companies are now actively seeking compliance solutions that are comprised of proven, scalable technologies that can be rapidly deployed and modified to address both current and future regulatory requirements. These solutions require enterprise-class content and process management capabilities to enable a much more comprehensive and value-driven approach to ensuring compliance.

FileNet Corporation helps organizations make better decisions faster by managing the content and processes that drive their business. FileNet's Enterprise Content Management (ECM) solutions allow customers to build and sustain competitive advantage by managing content throughout their organizations, automating and streamlining their business processes, and providing a spectrum of connectivity needed to enable critical and everyday decision-making.

FileNet ECM offers organizations a Compliance Framework that delivers control over critical business information through a combination of content, process and connectivity. While Content Management provides both enhanced visibility and control over critical information, Business Process Management drives the very processes that comprise an organization's compliance efforts. When employed in conjunction with FileNet's Compliance Framework that includes comprehensive records management and email management capabilities, FileNet ECM provides an effective and scalable platform for compliance.

- FileNet Email Manager is designed to help organizations capture, organize, monitor, retrieve, retain and share email content to improve business decision-making and support compliance. FileNet Email Manager's rules-based technology takes an intelligent approach to determining the value of an email's content. Rather than simply storing every email, FileNet Email Manager applies predetermined business rules at the server level to automatically assign the proper lifecycle criteria, enabling the automated enforcement of compliance with limited user interaction or user-related errors.

- FileNet Records Manager provides capabilities to administer the lifecycle of critical records, enforce processes for records management, respond to audits and inquiries, and demonstrate proof of compliance. The key differentiator in FileNet Records Manager is its innovative FileNet ZeroClick solution, which is designed to enforce records management policies at the technology layer, eliminating user-related error, time and cost factors, and ensuring best-practice records management.

In short, FileNet's Compliance Framework helps corporations to address today's regulatory requirements while effectively positioning them to rapidly respond to future legislation and the changing face of compliance. FileNet's Compliance Framework:

- Reduces the cost of compliance through process acceleration, automation, and instantaneous access to vital corporate content

- Enhances corporate transparency, providing top-down visibility into critical compliance processes, information, and controls

- Enables enterprise-wide contribution to compliance efforts, proactively managing the build, approval, and reporting of required information

- Reduces the risk of fines, penalties, and litigation resulting from non-compliance

- Enables organizations to be more responsive by immediately identifying and reacting to material events.

- Enhances business continuity and fail-over capabilities

- Ensures that vital corporate records, including email messages, are effectively declared, securely maintained, and properly destroyed at the end of their lifecycle

Hewlett-Packard Company

® 3000 Hanover Street
Palo Alto, CA 94304
800-637-7740
ilm-info@hp.com
www.hp.com/go/ilm-compliance

Putting information to work

HP provides a wide range of solutions designed to help companies achieve sustained compliance with industry and government regulations, specifically the Sarbanes-Oxley Act of 2002. The HP Sustained Compliance initiative addresses these new regulations and standards via a combination of technologies, strategies and services: HP Information Lifecycle Management (ILM), HP Information Technology Services Management (ITSM), HP Identity Management (IdM), and HP Business Process Management (BPM).

Regarding data retention, HP ILM provides a comprehensive strategy for perpetually managing and retaining all forms of digital information, including: email and instant messages; office documents; medical images that apply to related business issues and costs; audit requirements; protection against litigation; discovery requests; and corporate policy requirements. HP can help organizations comply with a broad range of regulatory mandates including Sarbanes-Oxley, SEC/NASD, Basel II, Solvency II, HIPAA, UK FSA's Policy Statement 04/09, German GDPDU and other industry regulations with customer-managed systems.

HP StorageWorks Reference Information Storage System (RISS) is an ILM archiving solution that converts data into information that can be searched via application-aware, context-based indexing and search tools. Unlike competing solutions, HP RISS integrates all of the required hardware, software and services that will provide a cost-effective and long-term storage of reference information. The solution architecture supports linear scalability without loss of performance by intelligently distributing terabytes of content across a grid of storage smart cells.

Another component within the HP ILM portfolio, HP StorageWorks File System Extender (FSE), is a cost-effective solution for managing massive amounts of file system stored data across storage tiers. Operation is automatic and transparent, increasing data management efficiency while reducing storage costs. Policies are defined to identify files for movement from the production storage to the secondary storage media. Rules are typically created to maintain active data on the high-performance production storage systems and move inactive data to the lower cost secondary storage. When combined with HP Write-Once, Read-Multiple (WORM) Ultrium tape and HP Ultra Dense Optical (UDO) WORM devices, FSE provides WORM file system, ensuring the non-tamperability of compliance records in a tiered storage environment.

Through HP ILM Compliance Services, HP consulting experts ensure that customers maximize the value of HP solutions by properly analyzing the customer's situation, creating a solution tailored to the customer's need, integrating the solution, and following up with audits and training.

The HP ILM services portfolio offers data classification consulting, legacy data reload and retrieval for a quick accessibility, industry partnerships and knowledge of industry best practices, providing a powerful solution that helps firms mitigate the risks of non-compliance while improving productivity and lowering the Total Cost of Ownership for sustained compliance.

With regard to Sarbanes-Oxley, HP is a recognized leader in regulatory compliance, and through its HP ITSM, HP IdM and HP BPM solutions, is helping companies not only meet these new regulations, but strive toward sustained compliance. HP ITSM addresses key IT processes impacted by regulatory requirements and provides auditable proof of compliance. HP Services experts use industry best practices such as ITIL to assess, document and implement IT process quality improvements. Use of HP IdM allows enterprises to mitigate risk and enforce compliance relating to identity and access management through secure audits of business processes and management of the relationship lifecycle. HP BPM helps organizations model and document business processes using industry-standard frameworks and best practices, as well as identify areas of non-compliance and process improvement. HP works with an organization's legal and financial partners to implement recommended process and IT improvements.

HP's multiple-prong, process-based standards approach to Sarbanes-Oxley compliance includes utilization of ITSM Infrastructure-Based Controls, which are supported by HP OpenView Management Software. HP OpenView provides a broad range of solutions which directly and indirectly support the Internal Controls outlined by the Committee of Sponsoring Organizations (COSO) and required by Sarbanes-Oxley. The strength and focus of HP OpenView and HP Services around IT Service Management and Identity Management serves as the basis for addressing a variety of internal controls, including Control and Monitor User Access, Financial Process Integrity and Section 802: Record Retention.

With HP's extensive technology and services portfolio, industry partnerships and knowledge of industry best practices, HP is unmatched in its ability to provide solutions for sustained compliance to companies of all sizes.

Kofax

16245 Laguna Canyon Rd
Irvine, CA 92618
Tel: 949-727-1733
Fax: 949-727-3099
Web: www.kofax.com
Internet: info@kofax.com

At Kofax, we focus on one critical business need: Making your business processes faster, more automated and less costly through information capture: collecting documents from throughout your organization, transforming them into useful information, and delivering it into your vital business systems.

Kofax is the world's leading provider of information capture solutions. No other company has the same global reach, depth of experience, or breadth of technology devoted to capturing business information—whether it originates on paper or in electronic files, in forms or in unstructured documents, in a single department or at remote offices throughout the world. Our products are widely used in insurance, finance, government, transportation, healthcare, and a broad range of other organizations that must process high volumes of documents and forms.

ADP turned to Kofax to expand their business process outsourcing business for stock brokerages. Kofax technology enabled ADP to process 2 million pages of new account documents every month for seven stock brokerages in multiple countries. The Kofax solution eliminated the need to ship paper documents and dramatically reduced the time and cost of processing new accounts.

Rent-A-Center turned to Kofax to automate their accounts payable process. Kofax technology enabled Rent-A-Center to automatically capture tens of thousands of invoices every week into their ERP system for quick turnaround and payment. The Kofax solution drove down the amount of manual data entry required and increased their ability to qualify for early payment discounts, resulting in an ROI of less than 12 months.

FedEx turned to Kofax to accelerate the processing of paper airbills. Kofax technology simplified the scanning process and improved the quality of scanned images, enabling FedEx to scan more than 1 million paper airbills every day at hundreds of offices around the world, The Kofax solution eliminated the need to ship the paper airbills, reduced the processing time from days to hours, and remains the world's largest distributed capture system.

The State of New Mexico turned to Kofax to preserve and enable easier public access to records. Kofax technology enabled the state's Oil Conservation Division to take millions of documents scattered across the state in hundreds of file cabinets and transform them into electronic images for public access through the web. The Kofax solution makes it easy for the agency's remote offices to scan hundreds of thousands of new documents into the archive every year.

With more than 75,000 seats sold across more than 15,000 installations, we've learned a lot about the critical factors that our customers consider when selecting a capture solution and a capture provider. In 2004 alone, Kofax customers purchased licenses to process more than 8.5 billion page images. Why? Our capture solutions are focused on our customers' critical needs:

- We offer the strongest integration with devices that collect business documents, such as scanners, multi-function peripherals (MFPs) and electronic sources such as XML streams.

- We have developed unsurpassed technologies for automatically transforming your documents into valuable information through separation, classification, extraction, and validation.

- We provide the widest integration with the business systems that need your captured information, such as ERP systems, CRM systems, enterprise content management systems, corporate databases and workflow systems.

- We have created an enterprise platform that is unmatched for high availability, adherence to standards, centralized management, process scalability, customizability, upgradeability, and its ability to be deployed across a widely distributed business environment.

- We deliver information capture solutions with some of the lowest total cost-of-ownership models in the industry.

- We lead our industry through innovation and a commitment to solving real business problems.

Ask our customers. Read our real-world case studies of major systems in a variety of industries. Or simply let our solutions prove themselves: Stand up a Kofax system side-by-side with any alternative solution and run them with your own documents. You'll find out what our customers already know. For information capture, Kofax is the answer.

Mobius Management Systems, Inc.

120 Old Post Road
Rye, NY 10580
tel 800-235-4471 / 914-921-7200
fax 914-921-1360
info@mobius.com
www.mobius.com

Mobius is the leading provider of **total content management** solutions that support regulatory compliance, automate business processes and integrate content across the enterprise. ViewDirect® TCM is a comprehensive suite that is unique in several important dimensions:

- *Breadth of functionality.* ViewDirect® TCM includes enabling software that meets all enterprise content requirements, including content integration, e-mail and records management, Web content management, document management, digital asset management, workflow and imaging, enterprise report distribution, and a compliance facility that ensures the accuracy of enterprise information.

- *Breadth of content.* ViewDirect TCM supports content in any format from any source, transforms it for multi-channel delivery and distributes it throughout the enterprise and beyond.

- *Scalability.* ViewDirect TCM scales from the desktop to the enterprise. Implementations range from departmental applications to multi-server systems with tens of thousands of users and billions of documents.

For over twenty years, Mobius has defined and led the market for software that stores, indexes, and distributes diverse information in any format from any source. Since 1981, Mobius has pioneered or advanced virtually every breakthrough in the evolution of technology for high-volume storage and distribution of diverse documents, reports and images. Mobius solutions have achieved industry-wide recognition for their ability to support high-volume, high-performance, simultaneous-access requirements in distributed environments that range from the desktop to the enterprise.

Integrating Content across the Enterprise

The Mobius vision is based on the view that both "human-created" content—generated by desktop applications—and "application-created" content—generated by production systems—is needed to fuel next-generation Web-based applications. Mobius sees the underlying architecture not as a long-term repository of infrequently accessed documents but rather as a scalable high-volume, rapid-access engine that transforms any type of unstructured data into the appropriate format and makes it available for real-time Web delivery and to support internal business processes.

In most organizations this broad diversity of content—bills, statements, check images, reports, scanned forms, e-mail, transactions, policies, customer correspondence, Web elements, audio, video and more—is dispersed throughout the global enterprise in various content repositories, databases, e-mail applications, and file systems. Content integration—via a single, integrated repository or via access to multiple, disparate repositories—is at the heart of ViewDirect TCM and enables a host of activities that leverage enterprise content.

Automating Business Processes to Streamline Operations

ViewDirect TCM includes solutions that address specific business issues. Often focused within a particular industry, these solutions integrate content, data and applications to automate the internal and external processes that connect employees, customers, partners and suppliers. Whether these applications automate the processing of policies, loans, deposits, checks and e-statements or Web-enable content for agents or supplier extranets, the benefits are similar: eliminating paper, mailing and data entry; expediting decision-making; streamlining business-critical operations; and enhancing customer service and partner relationships.

Managing Exploding Regulatory Requirements

Documents, records, e-mail, financial reports—all are subject to new levels of scrutiny and accountability and new standards for creation, handling and retention. ViewDirect TCM offers many ways to minimize corporate risk, from automating the collection, verification, audit, balancing and reconciliation of financial information across all applications and platforms to robust facilities for e-mail and records management that ensure capture, processing, archiving, access and disposition according to organizational and regulatory requirements.

Mobius products are used by leading companies across all industries worldwide, including more than sixty of the Fortune 100.® ViewDirect TCM, the most comprehensive suite of content management solutions available, helps these companies achieve a broad range of business objectives from improving operational productivity to leveraging the Internet for competitive advantage while protecting the bottom line.

About the Authors

Randolph A. Kahn, ESQ.

Randolph A. Kahn is an attorney and internationally recognized authority on the legal, compliance, risk management, retention, and policy issues of business information, information technology, electronic evidence, and records management. As founder and principal of Kahn Consulting, Inc. (www.KahnConsultingInc.com), Kahn leads a team of consultants who advise corporations and governmental agencies on a wide range of issues related to Information Management Compliance. He has played an important role in the development of industry standards related to e-records, electronic business risk management, information security, and information management. Each year, Kahn conducts dozens of seminars and training programs for corporate and government institutions. He is an instructor at George Washington University and a columnist for an information technology magazine. Kahn has authored numerous articles for legal, industry and mainstream publications and is regularly interviewed by a wide variety of media outlets. Kahn is the co-author of *Information Nation: Seven Keys to Information Management Compliance,* published in 2004 and *E-Mail Rules: A Business Guide to Managing Policies, Security, and Legal Issues for E-Mail and Digital Communication,* published in 2003. Mr. Kahn is the 2004 recipient of the Britt Literary Award.

Mr. Kahn may be contacted at rkahn@KahnConsultingInc.com or 847-266-0722.

Barclay T. Blair

Barclay T. Blair is a consultant and internationally acclaimed speaker and author specializing in the compliance, policy, and management issues of information technology. Mr. Blair advises Global 2000 companies, software and hardware vendors, and government agencies on a broad range of information management compliance issues. Mr. Blair is an executive editor of the *American Bar Association's PKI Assessment Guidelines*, participated in the development of a protocol for secure, digitally signed documents, and is the author of a draft ISO standard addressing long-term electronic records preservation. Mr. Blair has written and edited dozens of publications, speaks internationally on information management compliance matters, and is an instructor at George Washington University. Prior to *Information Nation Warrior,* Mr. Blair co-authored *Information Nation: Seven Keys to Information Management Compliance* and edited and contributed to several books, including: *Email Rules* (AMACOM Books: 2003); *Secure Electronic Commerce* (Prentice Hall: 2001); *Beginning XML* (Wrox: 2000); and *Professional XML* (Wrox: 2000). Mr. Blair is Director of the Technology Compliance Practice at Kahn Consulting, Inc.

Mr. Blair may be contacted at: bblair@KahnConsultingInc.com or 403-234-9347.